THE WOMEN WHO DANCED BY THE SEA

THE WOMEN WHO DANCED BY THE SEA

Finding Ourselves in the Stories
of our Biblical Foremothers

MARSHA PRAVDER MIRKIN, PH.D.

MONKFISH BOOK PUBLISHING COMPANY
RHINEBECK, NEW YORK

For information contact Monkfish Book Publishing Company, 27 Lamoree Road Rhinebeck, New York 12572

Library of Congress Cataloguing-in-Publication Data

Mirkin, Marsha Pravda, 1953-.
The women who danced by the sea : finding ourselves in the stories of our biblical fore-mothers / by Marsha Mirkin.
    p. cm.
Includes bibliographical references.
ISBN 0-9749359-0-5
1. Women in the Bible. 2. Bible. O.T.--Psychology. 3. Conduct of life. I. Title.
BS1199.W7M57 2004

20040112994

Portions of the chapter "The Women of Early Exodus" originally appeared in "All the Women Followed Her: A Collection of Writings on Miriam the Prophet and the Women of Exodus", published by Rikudei Miriam Press, 2521 Valleywood Dr., San Bruno, CA 94066.
The author wishes to acknowledge Tomy Redner for his kind permission to use Marion Weinberg's chapter from this same volume as well as stories about him and his children.

This book's epigraph is from the song "Water From Another Time" © 1985 by John McCutcheon.

Cover art, "Dance" by Marc Chagall
©2004 Artist Rights Society (ARS), New York / ADAGP, Paris

Book and cover design by Georgia Dent

Bulk purchase discounts, for educational or promotional purposes are available. Contact the publisher for more information.

First edition

First impression

In order to protect confidentiality, all characters in this book (except where noted) have been significantly altered and names changed or are composites of several altered cases.

Monkfish Book Publishing Company
27 Lamoree Road Rhinebeck, New York 12572
www.monkfishpublishing.com

This book is dedicated to Mitch, my husband and soulmate,
and to our two daughters, Allie and Jessy,
who have opened my eyes to the blessings in every moment.

I also dedicate this book to the memory of my beloved parents, Sidney and Ann Pravder, who imbued within me a love of Torah, and to the memory of my dear friend Marion Weinberg, a woman who danced by the sea.

"It don't take much, but you gotta have some
The old ways help the new ways come
Just leave a little extra for the next in line
They're gonna need a little water from another time."

—From *Water from Another Time* by John McCutcheon

Ackowledgments

I feel that it was possible to write this book only because I was inspired throughout my life by so many family members, friends, colleagues, clergy, clients and students. My heartfelt thanks to my agent, Stephanie von Hirschberg and publisher, Paul Cohen. Stephanie's humor, professionalism, and perseverance got me through some of the more discouraging times, and she shared in my happiness during the exciting times. Paul combines a collaborative spirit and wonderful creative energy. My thanks are also extended to Georgia Dent for her beautiful book jacket design and editorial suggestions and to my copy editor Susan Piperato.

Nobody could ask for more supportive and professionally exciting colleagues than those I have at the Brandeis Women's Studies Research Center (WSRC). I want to thank Dr. Shulamit Reinharz, the Center's Director, for giving me the opportunity to research and write this book as a scholar at the WSRC. I also appreciate the generous input from my writer's group and other WSRC colleagues: Penina Adelman, Nancer Ballard, Emily Corbato, Cara Dunne-Yates, Barbara Greenberg, Dru Greenwood, Tracey Hurd, Sandy Jones, Elizabeth Mark, Naomi Myrvaagnes, Tema Nason, Betsy Peterson, Rosie Rosenzweig, Phyllis Silverman, and Ethel Morgan Smith.

A big thank you to Harriet Lerner, my dear friend and colleague who not only reviewed chapters and offered encouragement, but also introduced me to Stephanie. Her own writing is an inspiration to me. My gratitude can't be put into words to my beloved friends Jodie Kliman and Mona Fishbane who went over this manuscript so carefully and offered such valuable feedback. A thank you is also extended to Lori Lefkovitz, Noam Zion and Silvia Barack Fishman for their feedback on the manuscript.

I would also like to thank Rabbi Alan Ullman, my teacher and friend, who confirmed for me that alternative understandings of Torah not only are possible, but also that I have the responsibility within our tradition to discover some of these understandings. Rabbi Ullman and I discussed the chapter on Eve and Adam in detail before it was written, and he also shared a number of ways of thinking about biblical characters, meanings of names, and interpretations of language.

My beliefs and my writing are strongly influenced by the work of multicultural and feminist family therapists. I have also been influenced by narrative therapists and by my colleagues at the Jean Baker Miller Institute whose work on the relational-cultural model made it possible for me to read Torah through that lens. A special thanks to Jan Surrey for her reviews of the early chapters of this book.

Rabbi Harold Kushner's book *How Good Do We Have to Be?* offers an interpretation of the Eve and Adam story that I found supported and deepened my own work. My work on Sarah, Hagar and Abraham expanded on ideas that I had begun to develop in a chapter I wrote for G.T. Reimer and J.A. Kates in their 1997 *Beginning Anew: A Woman's Companion to the High Holy Days.* NY: Touchestone Publishers.

A very special thank-you to two incredible Brandeis graduates, Ricki Wovsaniker and Elana Safer. As part of a the WSRC Student-Scholar partnership, they reviewed all the sources and footnotes, and discussed book chapters with me.

I would also like to thank the clergy at Temple Beth Elohim, Cantor Jodi Sufrin and Rabbis Joel Sisenwine, Jeff Lazar, Michele Lenke, and David Wilfond, for providing a spiritual home during the time I was writing this book and to Rabbi Sue Levi Elwell who helped me get started in this field.

I am indebted to the students and workshop participants who welcomed this material, and through their insights challenged me to expand my thinking. This is a much better book because of them. My appreciation to Dean Abby, Mary Dailey, Joyce Krensky, Bernice Lerner, and the other program and workshop coordinators who early on invited me to present my work to their communities and whose communities have been such a blessing to me as I continue to pursue this sacred work.

I could not have written this book without the help of all the individuals and families with whom I worked during my years as a clinician. They taught me much about struggle, love, resilience, and change.

Marion Weinberg of blessed memory, and her daughters Jessica and Gabrielle, inspired the chapter on Miriam. Their spiritual strength and ability to celebrate life is an inspiration.

I also want to honor my parents, Ann Goldman Pravder and Sidney Pravder. Both my mom and dad passed away during the time I was writing this book. My parents implanted within me a profound love for Torah and for Judaism. My mom taught me that social action needs to go hand in hand with study while my dad showed me that it is so important to appreciate all the blessings on our journey.

Finally, with great love and gratitude, thank you to my husband and daughters. Mitch patiently read and reread enough drafts to make anybody tired of this book, but he was always encouraging, excited, and right there to support me. I couldn't ask for a more loving and understanding life partner. Allie and Jessy are true inspirations. Thank you for teaching me so much about joy, love, insight and possibility, and for helping me to learn so much about myself and my relationships. The three of you are a profound blessing.

Table of Contents

There are many translations of the Hebrew Bible, and given the ambiguity and multiple possible meanings of a number of biblical words, translation is interpretation. The translation most often used in this book is the Jerusalem Bible, Koren Publishers.

Introduction

As a psychologist, I have had the privilege of working with the women, men, and children who allowed me to enter their struggles, their difficult loves, and their longings. They permitted me to both bear witness and actively share their despair, joy, bitterness and hope. I discovered that often I was journeying with them as they chose to leave their place of emotional enslavement, enter their psychological wilderness, and travel haltingly and with many detours toward their own Promised Land. The lessons about family and community that I learned from the psychotherapy relationship provided the template through which I began to interpret the Hebrew Bible. From this experience emerged "The Women Who Danced by the Sea," a new reading of stories in the Hebrew Bible that applies family therapy concepts and relational psychology,[1] the psychology of connections and disconnections between people, to narratives of biblical women.

My relationship with Torah began years before I had ever come into contact with the word "psychologist." Forty years ago, I sat in a second grade classroom in a small yeshiva[2] in Brooklyn, New York and began to read the book that would change my life forever. In Miss Baer's tiny classroom, surrounded by the smells of our bagged tunafish sandwiches, the calls of the kindergartners from the narrow, concrete yard below, and the gentle smile of my beloved teacher, we began to read Bereshit, the first book of Torah. And I fell in love. The stories came alive before me. They made me want to laugh and cry, they made me feel secure with my God and my people, they made me question, and they disturbed me. Perhaps my love and unease developed because in our little school, Miss Baer not only accepted even the most challenging questions, she also pushed us to ask and then to try to find a way to answer. She wove together what our rabbis said and what our seven-year-old minds tried to sort out. She valued God and Torah, and she valued us.

But she also left me with many unsettling questions, and more and more accumulated as my studies continued. I had eaten candy that mommy told me not to touch, but she didn't throw me out of the house. Why did God throw Adam and Eve out of Eden for eating the apple? Miss Baer told me that God was kind and gentle, so why did God ask Abraham to kill his child? Would my parents kill me if God requested that from them? Didn't God love children? When my friend and I had an argument in my apartment, Mommy and Daddy didn't send her home. They told me to work it out with her. Yet, when Sarah didn't get along with Hagar, Abraham sent Hagar away. I wouldn't want even an enemy's child to suffer the heat and thirst of the wilderness. Why would Abraham do that to his own wife and son?

As a teenager, I had more ability to think abstractly than I did when I was seven, and I could have begun to wrestle with those questions, but by that time I felt estranged from Judaism and from my cherished text. After all, I couldn't lead the prayers in my orthodox school[3] because I was a girl, even though I knew them inside out and would have done a much better job than Shmuel or Itzy. Then, when I turned thirteen, I didn't have a Bat Mitzvah because in my conservative tradition and my grandparents' orthodox tradition, girls weren't able to read Torah aloud from the bima (the raised platform from which Torah is read in many synagogues). Even when I turned to reform prayerbooks, the God in whose image I was made was always called He or Lord[4]. I could no more identify with a male Lord than I could with Henry VIII. I felt left out. When I made my last adolescent effort to reconcile with my Judaism, I enrolled in an after-school Hebrew High School Torah study. There, all the biblical heroes we studied were men. When my foremothers were mentioned, they were described as tempting men, deceiving men, competing shamelessly, or speaking out wrongly against men. When I was told during the Shabbat (Sabbath) blessing that I should grow up to be like Sarah, Rebecca, Rachel and Leah, I didn't know anything that felt meaningful about these women. I hadn't claimed them as my own. I didn't know it then, but during that time I felt like Hagar banished to the wilderness, I felt like Miriam sitting outside the Hebrew camp after being expelled for seven days.[5] And, without that knowing, I was becoming more and more estranged from my beloved Torah. Although, as we all know, we carry with us those we once loved, those we might love again, even during periods of estrangement.

My development as a psychologist, and particularly as a relational and cultural family therapist, was a journey that would eventually lead me back to Torah. I was drawn to relational therapy, particularly the ideas that growth occurs in the context of relationships and that the cornerstones of mental health are mutuality, empathy and authenticity. Through the years, this model has guided me in my clinical practice. I also identified with family therapy from early in my career, when it was far from mainstream psychology, because it took the locus of the problem away from the individual and placed it in the relationships among people and between people and their society. I was excited at the prospect of looking at people in the context of their lives, and supporting them as they worked toward overcoming their pain and suffering.

As I settled into my psychotherapy practice and my children began Hebrew school, I once again became engaged in the study of

Torah. I was in a different place than I had been so many years earlier. Through my practice, I had observed more about what happens when couples do not empathically connect, when insufficient attention is paid to the needs of children, when people take huge risks at tremendous cost to change their lives for the better, when someone maintains hope through what appears to be a hopeless situation, when truly hearing one another is transformative. With this life experience, I went back to the Torah and reread it carefully, knowing that there was a filter I was now placing atop the text that couldn't help but direct my understanding of it. I reread it as an adult who wanted to own it as my own and understand it so that it could move me, mold me, transform me. I reread it wanting to learn but unwilling to settle for only the male-discovered, ancient interpretations. I wanted to respect what the rabbis of our tradition have said over the past two thousand years, but also to recognize that they spoke from their experience, their time, and their society. If our Holy Book could survive all these years, if it is going to survive long after I'm gone, then it has to resonate with each of us, across gender, race, class, ethnicity, and across time.

In the anguish of a young woman who had to make a very risky choice in order to have more passion and intimacy in her life, I saw Eve holding the fruit of the Tree of Knowledge, moments before the bite. In the struggles of a wife who felt unheard and the husband who felt devoted and misunderstood, I saw the encounters between Sarah and Abraham. In the cries of a young Mexican-American woman who wanted to hold her ethnicity in a country that marginalized her for it, I saw Hagar. And as I kept studying the words of Torah and the words of our commentaries, as I grappled with ways of resonating with its teachings, and as I developed as a psychologist, the idea for this book was born.

Just as the individuals and families with whom I worked

brought me to Torah, so this psychological reading of Torah brought me to a richer understanding of individuals and families. I read about the Exodus from Egypt, understood how hard it is for us to leave our internal places of enslavement, and studied carefully how the Hebrews managed to leave, even though they often stumbled along the way. This interpretation helped me develop more patience and respect for the process of psychotherapy, the journey of change. I admired Miriam as she chose to dance after an awesome, traumatizing, life altering event and I recognized from her story that although we can't choose our fate, we can choose how we deal with it. I followed Hannah's movement from silence to a small internal voice to a resilient world-altering voice, and I understood more about working with the powerlessness and voicelessness that some women were experiencing when they came to work with me.

As a therapist, I have always tried to be attentive to the contexts of my practice and aware of my race and class privilege. In one hand, I hold my experiences as a white, economically privileged therapist. In my other hand I hold my experiences as a woman and as a Jew, and remembered the times I felt invisible, pushed out, discounted because of my gender or my religion. I felt both grateful for and challenged by the work of multicultural and feminist family therapists whose focus on social justice, honoring difference, empowerment, and understanding the impact of the larger societal context on individuals and families profoundly affected me personally and professionally. Because context is central to my practice, I developed an awareness that helped me interpret how marginalization and otherness might be explored in Torah. Hagar, a handmaid, a woman with no rights, a worshipper of Egyptian gods who had no place in the Hebrew community, was seen and heard by the Hebrew God and developed a covenantal relationship with the Eternal One. The fate of the entire Hebrew nation may have rested in the hands of three non-Hebrews, two midwives[6] and an Egyptian princess, and they modeled for us the ethics that we would later adopt at Sinai. The narratives of the strangers in our midst, or of those who judged us as strangers in their midst, were reflected in the stories brought to me by clients. These clients helped me pull meaning from the biblical stories, and those stories in turn guided me as I worked with clients who were marginalized in our society.

The purpose of this book is to explore stories of biblical women through the lens of psychology in an effort to cull meanings that promote our fullest emotional, spiritual and social development and support both our growth-in-relationship and Tikkun Olam (a Hebrew expression meaning the healing of the world). Each chapter delves into the life of a female character and her relationship with her loved ones and God. To do this, I use the age-honored method of understanding Torah known as "midrash." Where Torah is purposely ambiguous, with large white spaces between one word and another that beg for interpretation, midrash fills in those white spaces. It is the method our tradition uses to interpret Torah. As Barry Holtz writes,[7] "Sacred texts, most notably the Bible, are carefully interpreted, both to derive points of law and to give occasion for theological statements or stories and parables... Midrash comes to fill in the gaps, to tell us the details that the Bible teasingly leaves out...." While much of midrash was edited and written down between 400-1200 CE, the oral tradition of midrash began earlier and continues through this very day.

Today, there is a new excitement about midrash as a literary form of interpreting and understanding Torah in contemporary times. Because much of the new midrash is by and about women,[8] it is easy to believe that the traditional midrash is patriarchal or outdated. While some traditional midrash can certainly be misogynist as well as xenophobic,[9] it is exciting to discover the very progressive understandings that some of our sages had of women as well as of "the stranger" in our midst.[10] "The Women Who Danced by the Sea" develops new midrash based on a close textual reading, but it also taps understandings of Torah that date back to rabbinic and medieval times.

The concept of midrash is very similar to the idea of "storying" in current narrative theories of psychology.[11] This literature suggests that there is no single truth, but rather that we make meaning by constructing stories of our life experiences. Some of these stories are more privileged in our culture, and some of these stories are marginalized. The idea that adolescence is a time of separation and individuation is a dominant story in North American culture, while the concept that we grow interdependently within relationship is marginalized. Similarly, the stories of dominant white, upper middle class culture are given more credibility than the cultural stories of low-income people of color. Just as the dominant stories are shifting in psychology, understandings of Torah can also shift so that stories of women join men in the forefront of our tradition, and so that our interpretations can include the values of interdependence, relationship, and honoring difference.

The central theme of this book is that we yearn to be in meaningful relationships, and yet we stumble in our efforts to form, maintain and grow in these relationships. Each chapter looks at a different foremother and at a different issue she must grapple with in order to move into deeper relationship with herself, those she loves, and the Divine. Each chapter ties those struggles to our own contemporary problems, and looks at both what we can learn from the experiences of our foremothers and how we can understand our foremothers based on our own life experiences. Their legacies can guide us—woman and man, Jew and non-Jew, religiously affiliated and unaffiliated—as we make similar mistakes, have similar sorrows and confusions, and find similar hope and blessings on our paths to more intimate connection.

Notes

1. Jean Baker Miller, Irene Stiver, Judith Jordan, Janet Surrey and their colleagues at the Wellesley College Stone Center developed the relational model and the concepts of mutuality, empathy and authenticity.

2. The yeshiva is a place of study. In this context, it is an orthodox Jewish day school.

3. Judaism has four major denominations: reform, reconstructionist, orthodox and conservative. Each of these denominations encompasses a spectrum of beliefs, so that while it may be necessary to define the denominations for those unfamiliar with them, I do it with the caveat that it is impossible to accurately portray them in a few sentences. Orthodox views the Torah as the immutable word of God, the embodiment of the divine mind and will. The Jewish legal tradition known as "halakhah" is seen as inspired by God and therefore binding (although even in the modern Orthodox tradition, there is a procedure for rethinking halakhic rulings). Halakhah leads the orthodox Jews in a way of life that is an all-encompassing commitment to fulfilling "Mitzvot" (the 613 divine commandments written in Torah). The conservative movement is "characterized by its loyalty to tradition and openness to change based on a rigorous examination of Jewish sources and historical development. On the one hand, the Conservative movement insisted that halakhah is binding. On the other hand, the Conservative movement found within Jewish history a process of evolution…It tried to walk a fine line between …an uncritical acceptance of the Jewish past and…a radical rejection of that past."(Simcha Kling, *Embracing Judaism*, revised by Carl M Perkins, Rabbinical Assembly: 1999, p. 39). Reform Judaism was the pioneer liberal Jewish movement. It is guided but not governed by halakhah, sees revelation as

ongoing, emphasizes social action as the fulfillment of the Jewish religious mission in this world, and views mitzvot as spiritual exercises to train our souls to embrace social action (Personal communication, Rabbi David Wilfond, June, 2000). Reconstructionism, the newest of the major denominations, supports much of halakhah while assuming that not every word of Scripture is factual and divinely ordained. Reconstructionism emerged as the liberal branch of the conservative movement and the first Jewish egalitarian movement. As its founder, Mordecai Kaplan, said, referring to rabbinic law, "The ancients have a vote but not a veto." Reconstructionist prayer books delete references to Jewish chosenness, the Messiah, and hope for reinstitution of sacrifice (see for example the *Kol Haneshamah* prayer book, Reconstructionist Press, 1989).

4. Although God is understood in Torah to be without form and hence without gender, the Hebrew language is gendered. While I replace "Lord" (an English translation that may not correspond with the Hebrew word) with "Eternal" or "God," and attempt to use more inclusive language in both quotes and in referring to God, there are no English pronouns that can replace His with a gender-free form. Therefore, there are times when I directly quote from the Tanach using the male pronoun for God. I think this is unfortunate but I haven't found a solution to this dilemma. It is also important to note that there are also some feminine metaphors for God in the Tanach.

5. See Genesis 21:10-16 and Numbers 12:14-15.

6. Some commentators believe the midwives were Hebrew. The wording in Torah is ambiguous.

7. Holtz, Barry (1989). *Back to the Sources: Reading the Classic Jewish Texts*. NY: Simon and Schuster, p 179, 180.

8. There are many more books containing feminist midrash than can be listed here, but some examples include Kates, J. & Reimer, G. (1994). *Reading Ruth*. NY: Ballantine Books.; Reimer, G. & Kates, J. (1997) *Beginning Anew: A Woman's Companion to the High Holy Days*. NY: Simon & Schuster.; Rosenblatt, N. & Horwitz, J. (1995). *Wrestling with Angels: What Genesis Teaches Us About Our Spiritual Identity, Sexuality, and Personal*

Relationships. NY: Delta.; Frankel, E. (1996). *The Five Books of Miriam.* San Francisco, CA: Harper-Collins. A book that had a profound influence on me as I began this work is Plaskow, J. (1990). *Standing Again at Sinai.* San Francisco: Harper-Collins.

9. For example, Adam is said to have lost out as a result of having listened to his wife (Genesis Rabbah 19:6). Another midrash states that Adam was not initially moved to listen to Eve and bite from the forbidden tree, but Eve screamed until Adam finally listened to her (Genesis Rabbah 19:5). It is also said that before Moses was born, Miriam was a prophetess, but after he was born, prophecy was taken away from her and given to Moses (Exodus Rabbah, 15:20). Although the Torah said that God spoke to Hagar, midrash changes the story and instead says that God never spoke to any woman except for the righteous, so God must have spoken to the Egyptian handmaiden through an angel (Genesis Rabbah 45:10). All citations from midrash Rabbah are from the edition edited by Freedman, H. & Simon, M., London: The Soncino Press, 1961.

10. There are too many examples to list them all, but the following demonstrate the openness in some parts of our tradition to the equal role of women and to advocacy for those who are often maligned. Rabbi Samuel b. Nachman, 4th century, believed that the first earth being was not male but rather was both male and female created back to back and double-faced. Sarah, in Megillah 14b (Version of the Babylonian Talmud used in this text is edited by Rabbi Dr. I. Epstein , 1978, London: Soncino Press.) is said to see things through Divine Inspiration, and Ta'anis 9a (ibid) includes Miriam among the three good leaders of Israel (Moses and Aaron being the others). Esau, rather than being maligned as is typical in our tradition, was praised by Rabban Shimon b. Gamlilel who said "No man ever honored his fathers as I honored my fathers; but I found that Esau honored his father even more than I (Deuteronomy Rabbah, 1:15).

11. cf. White, Michael, *Re-Authoring Lives*, Adelaide, Australia: Dulwich Centre, 1995.

✠ *1* ✠

EVE: CHOOSING A LIFE WORTH LIVING

A PEACEFUL SADNESS interwoven with quiet energy seemed to emanate from Darlene. This would be her last therapy session with me, and she softly reviewed the road she had traveled, the road we had traveled together. For three years before she reached a decision, Darlene pondered divorcing her husband and childhood sweetheart Nick. She struggled painfully and doggedly, noting his kindness, noting that they had starting dating when they were sixteen, that in their forties they had collaborated well on raising their two teenagers. And yet, she had felt empty for so long. Not desperately unhappy, just empty. While Nick was kind, she didn't feel the resonance with him that she had when they married at age twenty. He listened patiently to her glowing attempts to discuss music, and he even accompanied her to several jazz recitals and absentmindedly commended her efforts to compose. But she was empty. She suggested couples therapy. He was surprised, but agreed. The polite remoteness was unaltered after a year of religiously attending sessions. Then one day, Darlene walked into my office with more energy radiating from her than I had ever seen before. She bumped down into a chair, looked me intently in the eyes, and told me that not only didn't she love Nick anymore, but she also just had a glimpse of what the world would be like if she weren't partnered with this sweet, ineffectual man in this boringly civil relationship. She talked about the opportunity to pursue her career in music, about a place where she could get a fellow-

ship to study further, about the freedom to take that on now that her younger son was starting college, about the model she was creating for her children about lifeless marriages, about her fear that her sons would emulate the unhappy passivity of their parents. She was moving out. Within a year, Darlene and Nick were divorced. When I saw Darlene during that first year, pain often contorted her face. She had to deal with her two angry sons, with her wounded former husband, with her own loss of a predictable relationship, with the insecurity of employment with no second salary to support her, with her own guilt at what she viewed as a betrayal of their childhood love.

But, the pain was tempered with a zest that I had never before seen in Darlene, with a knowledge that she was growing and laughing and hurting in a way that she hadn't experienced in so long that she did not even remember it was possible to have the intense experience of feeling, of being. She loved her work, she thrived on her music, she nourished close friendships, she patiently heard her sons' accusatory anger, she stretched, and she grew. Two years after ending therapy, Darlene entered a new relationship, not knowing how it would turn out, but knowing she felt more alive than she had in a long time. She had eaten from the tree of knowledge, and was propelled, excruciatingly, brilliantly, magnificently, into life.[1]

Most of us were taught that the story of Eve and Adam is a story of sin and punishment, even though neither of those words is ever used in this text[2]. Instead, perhaps we can begin to see the story of Eve and Adam as the story of our own development, and of the longing, desire, joy and tears that are born on our journey through life. Perhaps it can be understood as a story about what it means to be human, gloriously and fallibly human, and how we can make our lives a blessing. It is a story of partnership and parenting, of risk taking and losing and winning. This primordial tale can be the story of our own lives.

The first time that we hear about a human being in the Hebrew Bible is when God decides to make male and female in God's image.[3] This creation is named "Adam," or Earth Being. Because there is only one first creation, and because we are told that God created both male and female, some sages teach that this first person was created both male and female *within the same body*.[4] God then breathes the breath of life, the spirit of the Eternal, into the nostrils of this Earth Being, and Adam becomes a living soul. While our bodies had been created already, it is in this scene that our soul is born. It is God's breath—that spirit, that energy, that flow from the non-material world—that gives birth to our soul, the spirit and energy that gives meaning to our lives. While we were made out of the earth, this Living Soul, "Nefesh Chayah," connects us to the divine within each of us, enabling us to experience the emotional and spiritual parts of ourselves that so enrich our lives.

Once Adam has body and soul, God recites the first prohibition given to this newly formed Earth Being in the infancy of the human race: God tells this being not to eat from the Tree of Knowledge of Good and Evil, or else Adam will surely die. "Die" is so emphasized that God states it twice: "You will die die!"[5] Those of us who are parents understand God's emphasis on this early prohibition. We can remember telling our two-year-olds not to run into the street. We can remember being adamant about this prohibition, perhaps telling the toddler that we don't want her to be hurt by a car. At some point, though, this toddler will grow older and will crave the experience of crossing the street and wonder what's on the other side. At some point, that developmental push will be more powerful than our prohibition. But not yet, not while our child is

3

still a toddler and we are watching carefully to make sure that the prohibition isn't breached.

In Genesis, God takes on that role of a protective, knowledgeable parent. God knows what Adam at this point cannot comprehend: That there are risks, consequences, and uncertainty that go along with the knowledge of good and evil. Growing up means taking in knowledge that is both wonderful and frightening. We have to be developmentally ready to take on that knowledge of good and evil and not become overwhelmed and immobilized by what we see. Adam, in the childhood of humankind, was not.

God warns Adam that death is the consequence of eating from the Tree. But death does not have to be physiological. Another way of translating God's prohibition is "you will die a death." Whenever we take a growth-producing step, a step toward more wholeness, we also experience a loss, a death of sorts. Some part of our past, some piece of our innocence dies and we can't return to it. When my grandparents immigrated to America, they felt so lucky to raise their children in a country where they could safely practice their religion and have more economic opportunity than in their homeland, but they also had to mourn the loss of familiarity, of friends, of the smell of the fields in early morning, of familiar accents speaking familiar words. With that death came great possibility for life. But, they had to be ready to accept that death in order to open their eyes and hearts to the wonderful possibilities--that is the stuff that both heroism and everyday life is made of.

After warning Adam of the tree that this Earth Being is not yet prepared to encounter, God makes a critical observation of the human condition. God sees Adam surrounded by animals and lush vegetation, but without a friend or soul-mate, and observes that it is not good for a person to be alone. In these few words, "it is not good for Adam to be alone,"[6] a critical relational value is introduced to the world. Throughout the Hebrew Bible people are told not to be alone—partners and community are central to individual and communal development. We see this when Abraham is told to leave his father's house and the home of his birth, and yet he leaves with his wife and community. We see it when Moses returns to Egypt only when he is promised that his brother will go with him, and much later, when Ruth decides to accompany Naomi on her journey home. Being alone is not a value in this Holy Book.[7]

Most of us are familiar with the story that God took out one of Adam's ribs to form Eve. However, an alternative translation is that while the Earth Being slept, God separated the sides, and from one of the sides, Adam's partner was formed.[8] A male Adam then awoke, and called his partner "Isha," or woman. It was only after "Isha" was created that the remaining earth person was called "Ish," or man. Only after woman was created was it possible to become man for we define ourselves in relation to the others in our lives. This reading of the text counters the argument that man was created before woman, that woman is simply a piece of man, and that therefore man is superior. It also counters the argument that woman was created later than man and is therefore more highly evolved. Perhaps this story isn't about male or female superiority or inferiority. Perhaps the point of this story is that we can't understand who we are if we live isolated, independent lives. It is only in relationship with other people that we begin to understand ourselves, to become more self-aware, just as Adam understood himself to be man once he had a relationship with another human being.[9]

I remember when June and Linda came to my office, astonished by the argument they had been having all week. Both secular Jews, the couple had never thought much about their religion or heritage. At least they hadn't until June brought home a Christmas tree on December 21st. Linda was outraged, and then amazed at her outrage. Linda had thought that Judaism didn't matter to her. It wasn't so much that she rejected her religion; it was simply that she hadn't thought about it in many years. When June brought home the tree, Linda was furious and accused June of rejecting Judaism and acting Christian. June felt severely hurt and misunderstood. Although June hadn't participated in many religious rituals over the years, she felt some connection to Judaism, but she also had powerful, warm memories of her German-American Jewish family purchasing a Christmas tree each year and sharing together time and presents. To her, that tree represented family. Now that she and June were in a committed relationship, she wanted to share that warm, loving experience with her partner. As we discussed the meanings of the tree, each woman was able to recognize that the other's beliefs and reactions helped her to form and formulate her own convictions. They could begin to appreciate each other for helping to clarify each other's values and beliefs. After all, it was only when Adam called his partner isha/woman that he could recognize himself as ish/man.

Now the stage is set. We have two people in the Garden of Eden. We have all the animals living together peacefully and all the plants (except for the infamous one) at their disposal. The garden life is peaceful; God walks in this garden and people and God seem to have a personal relationship. But we don't hear any babies crying; we don't read about passionate longing or hugging or arguing or lovemaking. We know that people are made in God's image, but God is the Creator, and to be in that image, we too should be creating. Yet, once the man and woman are made into separate beings, neither creates anything. They exist. There is no poetry or music or art, no investigations on the nature of life, no children. In fact, no life-affirming decisions are being made at all. They are living, but without the passion, without the bursting creativity and hope that we experience when we feel fully alive, that Adam might have felt when he named the animals before he was split into two.

We are told that in the garden, during the childhood of humankind, the man and the woman are naked and without shame. I think of the photos my parents have of me at age two, gleefully naked on the beach. Not too many years later, I remember begging my parents to take those embarrassing pictures out of the album and tear them up. At the age of two, there is no knowledge of our own imperfection, no sense that others are judging us and that we won't measure up, no self-consciousness. This is the nakedness of Eden. And it doesn't last.

In the next verse, the woman, who after leaving the garden will be named Eve,[10] meets the serpent, and here begins a new chapter in the western cultural history of maligning women. Most of us learned that the woman interacts with the snake because she's more gullible, or more prone to sin, or less morally developed.[11] Women are then blamed for all life's misery because of Eve's inter-action with the snake and the fruit. Rarely is Eve portrayed with the courage and depth of understanding that she so boldly demon-strates. Perhaps the woman meets the snake precisely because she is developmentally ready to do so. After all, when do most children begin the process of growing up, and physically and emotionally catapulting toward adulthood? We are told that this begins at puberty, around seventh grade. Yet, if you look at a group of sev-enth graders, you will notice something that the Bible took into account: For a short time, the girls (on average) are often more physically and emotionally developed than the boys. Eve was maturationally prepared for her encounter with the serpent, so she had to lead the way.

The snake holds out to Eve the idea that if she were to eat of the forbidden fruit, she could be like God. She could be like the all-powerful, all-wise parent! Although the serpent entices Eve with the possibility of maturity and empowerment, the snake is unable to envision the consequences of the action. The snake tells Eve that she in fact won't die a death if she eats from the tree. How limited is the snake's vision! We see this as much today as in the dawn of humankind. Sex, for example, is such a lure for adolescents: It is the forbidden fruit with its promise of pleasure, maturity, and belonging. Yet, we also know that unprotected sex can lead to AIDS, pregnancy, STDs and a host of other problems; and that when people are emotionally unprepared for a sexual relationship, pain and hurt ensue. The serpent doesn't talk about that part. The serpent lures us with the pleasures while at the same time being incapable of predicting the problems that go hand in hand with the joys of adulthood. God, as we will see later, will be able to share with us the consequences of developing into mature human beings. God will help us understand that there is a death that we die whenever we move forward in life. The serpent, reflecting our single-minded desire for maturity and empowerment, can tell Eve only about the pleasures without the dangers inherent in moving to this next step in our development.

Yet Eve, even as she hears the enticing words from the serpent, does not casually or impulsively accept the lure. Her response to the serpent is that of a young person ready to enter the next phase of life. Eve neither goes along with the serpent, nor does she reject its enticement because her Parent told her not to eat the fruit. Instead, Eve uses all her expanding capacities to observe the situation and decide how it will impact her. She notices that the fruit is good for food, a desire for the eyes, and pleasant because it can make one enlightened. Eve notices that the forbidden fruit could sustain her intellectually, physically and aesthetically, and she wants that sustenance. The word "good" that is used by God during creation is also used to describe this fruit. Therefore, this fruit, if she is ready to eat it, can give her the opportunity to fulfill her potential and create/birth future generations. Pulled by the lure of growing into adulthood, aware of only the benefits and not the risks of maturity, she chooses to eat the fruit.

On that momentous day before Darlene came to my office and announced that she was leaving her marriage, she had been sitting in a restaurant with Nick, wordlessly drinking coffee as their two friends, also married for many years, bantered affectionately with each other. Darlene thought longingly of her friends' relationship, thought about the music fellowship, envisioned herself in a place where she could be nurtured emotionally, spiritually, and intellectually. She took a bite of the fruit and decided to leave the relationship. Later, she would have to deal with the challenges of angry children, a betrayed husband, confused parents, her own insecurities, and a very limited, competitive job market, but that was not what propelled her at that moment. The pre-knowledge, often viscerally sensed before spoken, of what will sustain us impels us to take risks, and Darlene, just like her first fore-mother, took a bite of the fruit.

With that bite, life as it was known changed forever, and people moved into being more full human beings, more adult human beings, forever grappling with the joys and sorrows inherent in all our choices. Eve had listened to her need for growth, she had reflected on the rightness of the decision; she had the courage to leave childhood behind and move toward adulthood. But, she hadn't yet begun to understand or even predict the loss attached to any major developmental step. Later, God would do that with her. In a powerful statement to all generations that followed her, Eve's very first act after choosing to gain knowledge of good and evil is to share the fruit with Adam. What makes us most human, most in accordance with God's decision to create two people, is being in relationship. God pronounced earlier that it is not good for Adam to be alone. Now, Eve acts in accordance with God's observation and her first action is to share the fruit/knowledge with Adam.

When an eminently successful man talked about independently pulling himself up from his bootstraps to become a highly educated and influential professional, he may have denied a critical piece of life-affirming knowledge: that he could never have truly done this on his own. A son of poor parents, this man had a mother and sister willing to work long hours in order to advance his education. Their dedication to their relationship with him made possible his fuller emergence as a successful professional. Just like Eve, this mother and sister made a self-conscious decision to act in a way that honors the relationship.

So both Eve and Adam take a bite of the fruit, and that early time when everything was simple and there was nothing to fear is lost. But, it is lost in the service of their development, in the service of actualizing life. The first loss occurs when self-acceptance is replaced by self-consciousness. We are told that the eyes of Adam and Eve were opened, and they knew that they were naked, and they sewed fig leaves together and made themselves loincloths. At some point we experience self-knowledge and realize that we're not perfect; that while we are made in God's image, we are not

God. That makes us very vulnerable, and we develop many strategies to hide our vulnerability. You can see these strategies at work
among children: When one child says, "I hate you," the targeted
child may respond, "Who cares?" But, of course he cares. He's
simply covering up his vulnerability as our foreparents covered
theirs. As adults, we want to tell another person that we love him/
her, but we fear the other person won't respond in kind, so we
silence ourselves. Again, we're covering our vulnerability with
silence, just as a newly self-conscious Eve and Adam tried to cover
themselves with fig leaves.

When they realize that God is approaching, their vulnerability and shame must skyrocket! After all, God knows everything so
God would know how flawed they are! (After all, with knowledge
they are now self-conscious and even they could see their own
flaws.) So, they hide from God in whose eyes they know they are
imperfect.

*In a reconstruction of the words of a client who remembered
an interaction with her father:[12] "I was always daddy's girl,
and I thought I was perfect in his eyes. One day he told me I
was putting on a little weight. I felt so ashamed, so defective,
that I ran into my room and wouldn't come out. It was horri-
ble. To this day, whenever I think about that moment, I feel
fat and ashamed."*

Often, we feel ashamed when we feel we can't measure up,
and we cover our shame with defensiveness and both valid and
invalid excuses. We say that we don't play the piano as well as our
classmate because we don't have as much time to practice, or we
didn't get promoted because our boss would feel too threatened by
our competence, or we lost our tempers with a partner because the
partner provoked us. There is often some truth to these statements,

but they also cover up shame, much in the same way as Eve and Adam cover themselves when they notice their nakedness, and then cover their behavior when God speaks to them.

God asks Adam, "Where are you?...Who told you that you were naked? Did you eat from the tree which I commanded you not to eat from?"[13] Why would God bother to even ask these questions? Doesn't God know the answers? Think of that broken vase in the living room. The only person who had been in the living room was your five-year-old, and you heard the crash of the vase. The child then ran out of the room. You might say, "Where are you, Sam? Do you know the vase was broken? Did you break it?" with the hope that your child would own responsibility for the action. The broken vase, at that moment, is less important than imparting a sense of taking ownership for one's actions. Sometimes, when children are able to communicate their reasons for disobeying, our anger can dissipate. I remember that the first time that my daughter was allowed to walk to town with a friend, she came home twenty minutes later than our agreement. I was worried during that twenty minutes, and both relieved and angry when the bell rang. But, when she entered, she was able to tell me that she knew I was worried, but that since it was her first time in town she didn't realize how long it would take her to walk home, and that when she realized she was late, she stopped to call but the line was busy. How could I be angry at that responsible acknowledgement of her reasons for her behavior?

On the other hand, if she told me she was late because the friend convinced her to stay in town longer, I would certainly have remained angry. And so it was with Adam. Adam tells God that the woman *whom God created to be his partner* gave him the fruit. It reminded me of the time when, I am truly embarrassed to say, my fifth grade teacher asked me whether I was chewing gum and I said that Joann gave it to me. That statement certainly didn't get me off the hook—if anything, it made things worse. And Adam upped the ante by indirectly blaming God, by saying that the woman whom God created as his partner was responsible for the disobedience. I can imagine my teacher's reaction if I said "I got the gum from Joann, the girl whom you chose to sit next to me!"

God next turns to Eve with a different question: "What is this that you have done?"[14] God is not accusing Eve of disobedience, but rather is asking Eve to own and explain her behavior. God gives Eve latitude to behave responsibly and to present her case. Eve does not offer an explanation. She doesn't say that she saw she could be nourished aesthetically, physically, and intellectually by the fruit and so she decided to eat it. Instead, she immaturely responds that the serpent beguiled her. The road to maturity is not traversed in one step—or in one bite. It's a process, and Eve is at the beginning of the journey.

Now we hear the consequences of the move into adulthood; the potential joys and sorrows of growing up and being able to make the choice between a life that is full of love, passion, joy and pain, and one that is constricted. Once we are able to reason morally, life gets complicated. Our choices can cause us pain as well as exhilaration; desire is both a blessing and a challenge. When God speaks to Eve and Adam, God shares this full range of experience, both blessings and curses. Much later in Torah, God tells the Children of Israel that what is put before us can be a blessing or a curse,[15] and we need to take responsibility to live our lives as a blessing.

The first blessing-curse that God shares is that there will be pain in childbearing and sorrow in having children. Further, Eve will desire her husband who will rule over her. At first glance, this sounds like a harsh, sexist punishment. But yet, in my heart, I know that God would want us to gain knowledge and live our lives more fully. So why would God punish us? Where is the blessing in God's words and how can we understand the grim statements? Imagine Eve, who never had a human parent and never birthed a child, hearing not simply that she will bear children in pain but that she will bear children at all! This is the first moment that Eve finds out she will have children. While the original earthling was told to be fruitful and multiply, this did not happen within the confines of Eden. It takes a certain knowledge and maturity to responsibly parent. So it is only as a consequence of Eve biting the fruit that God gives Eve the most precious of gifts: the knowledge that she will have children. But we also know that while parenting may be the most awesome, meaningful part of our lives, there is sorrow and worry and anxiety and disappointment in parenting.[16] We never sleep as well again, we are never as free from fear again, the intensity of the joy and sorrow in our lives multiply beyond measure.

If God blesses us with the capacity to love so completely, we are very vulnerable and at some point we will be hurt. When we first become pregnant when we had so hoped to become pregnant, or hear that we will become adoptive parents after waiting so long for that phone call, we are joyous, and we are also immediately fearful. Will this fetus survive? Will this baby be healthy? Will the biological parents renege on the adoption? And that's just the beginning. When my clients told me about their fifteen-year-old who would not respond to curfews, hung out with the wrong crowd, and was using drugs, their anguish was palpable. But it doesn't have to be extreme behavior for us to feel the pain anticipated in this passage of Torah. When our children strive to become class officers and lose the election, or when they feel rejected by their friends, or strike out when the bases are loaded, we feel with them, and we hurt with them. When they cut us off with slammed doors or unbroken silences, the hurt we feel can be almost unbearable.[17]

While the information about children is directed toward Eve, Rabbi Kushner[18] argues that it is meant not only for Eve. He proposes that this directive includes Adam as much as the later statement to Adam that he will return to dust includes Eve. Just as woman isn't exempt from death just because the pronouncement was made to man, so man isn't exempt from the poignant experiences of parenting simply because he didn't give birth to the child. All parents who have ever longed for a child, be they female, male, adoptive, biological or step, resonate with the blessing of children and the pain and fear inherent in parenting.

But what about Adam ruling over Eve? While some people read these lines literally as the husband will be in charge of the wife, and others see these lines as a description of the sociopolitical reality of patriarchy,[19] I prefer to understand this as a statement of engagement. Again, God is sharing with us both the joy and pain of relationship. If we are intimately engaged with another, then we are ruled by our partner's needs as well as our own. Ruling over us means that we can no longer live independent lives, out of connection with others. This is an expansion of God's original statement that it is not good for Adam to be alone. Once we take the risk of being intimate, of engaging in relationship, there is a part of us that is freer than we have ever been before—that's the part that propelled Eve toward eating and sharing the fruit with her partner. There is also a part of us that is bound by the desires and the feelings of the other. Adam's feeling of "boundness" to Eve might have enabled him to take a bite of the fruit without any questions or hesitation simply because Eve was so excited about and desirous of sharing her newfound knowledge. The relationship and mutuality between partners creates both freedom and commitment and will be both our sustenance and our challenge in the world outside of Eden. Being ruled by our partners may be a small price to pay for intimacy, commitment, and mutual love, but God wants us to know that there is a price.

Then God addresses the man saying that because he listened to his wife and ate the fruit, he will have to work hard for his food. Further, just as he was made of dust, he will return to dust. Why is the pronouncement about work connected to the statement "because he listened to his wife"? In order to flourish outside of Eden, people are going to have to take initiative. When Adam eats the fruit, he shows that he can support his wife, but he doesn't yet show that he can evaluate a situation, join in a reflective decision making process, and thus take initiative. Adam doesn't ask Eve why she thought eating the fruit was a reasonable decision, and Adam doesn't check out the fruit himself and notice that it is aesthetically, emotionally, and intellectually pleasing. He just eats it. That passivity might be acceptable in Eden, but he needs more inspiration to live successfully in the outside world. So, he will need to think about how to make food grow in this stubborn soil, how to cultivate crops in a new environment. But, not only will he labor hard, he will also eat the herb of the field and the bread. So, through his creative work, Adam will be nourished. Although the work will be difficult, Adam may now discover that what is planted in difficulty can be reaped in satisfaction; what allows us creativity and passion can also be our most frustrating and disquieting experiences.

While this statement was made to Adam, all of us—male and female—can connect with it. *It is what makes Nydia continue to work in the lab even though she hasn't gotten the results she longs for. Year after year, she works in medical research and the disease is still not cured. While she feels discouraged, she also*

16

experiences hope and passion and creativity, and so she continues her work. The Bible doesn't just say that work will be difficult. The larger picture is "in the sweat of thy face, shalt thou eat bread."[20] Working the land is not simply a laborious exercise; it is a process through which benefits are reaped. In our own lives, that payoff is vitality, creativity, energy, excitement, and satisfaction with our labor.

For the first time, we are confronted with our mortality as we learn that we will return to dust. Before Eve and Adam eat the fruit, at a time when they live in comfortable, peaceful, undifferentiated Eden with no children, no passionate work, and no passionate love, they don't have to think about death. Part of our humanity is our mortality and part of our maturational process is our coming to terms with that mortality.

If we were lucky to be children or adolescents in an area that was not war-torn or bullet-torn or ravaged by illness or natural disaster, we rarely thought of our own death. Life seemed to stretch on indefinitely, and we didn't pay attention to the limitations of our time on earth. With maturation comes the knowledge that we are here for a limited time, and this too, as with all of God's other pronouncements, is a painful blessing. Often, knowing life has limits propels us to live each moment to its fullest and allows us to live creative, invested, relational lives. Adam seems to understand this, because the first thing he does after hearing that he will eventually die is to name his wife "Eve," which means the mother of all life, as if knowledge of death gave him insight into the meaning of life. She earns her name because through taking that bite, Eve gives us the opportunity to know, to choose passion and intimacy, to parent and raise children, to work creatively, and to leave something that continues even when we die.

Once God finishes telling Eve and Adam about the problems

and joys of a fuller life, God clothes them and sends them out of the garden.[21] God never abandons them, but rather helps them cover their vulnerability so that they can begin to face the challenges outside of Eden. God makes them coats of skin, which are more substantial than their fig leaves, thus better preparing them for their new lives. With the act of clothing Eve and Adam, God shares with us that growing up and leaving home isn't about relational cut-off. We and our children are capable of staying in relationship with each other throughout the life cycle, but as God shows us, we as parents have to be aware that what is helpful to our children changes at different developmental stages.

With the bite from the Tree of Knowledge, Adam and Eve leave the psychological space of childhood and enter a world ripe with possibility and danger. Outside of Eden, I imagine that Adam and Eve would share the pleasure of creating the first human being to be born from a human being. I imagine Eve suffering the excruciating pain of birthing her child that moves her to the inexpressively rewarding delight of seeing him for the first time, a reflection that the Tree is indeed good, that the fruit indeed offers a courageous Eve and her beloved Adam the possibility of taking part in creation. Soon she will find out more fully what God meant by the statement that there is pain with bearing children. Soon her son will break her heart. But my guess is that her children would also allow her to experience more joy, more depth of feeling, more emotional expansion than she ever dreamed possible during her stay in Eden. With her one dramatic, courageous bite of the fruit, she jumps head on into life, and to this day, because of Eve, we feel love and loss, hope and longing, passion and desolation.[22] Our first mother's action allows us to strive to once again walk with God, to aspire to live in God's image, and to experience more life than she ever could have imagined during that primordial time in the Garden. Would we have it any other way?

Notes

1. All vignettes in this book are either composites based on experiences with several clients or are significantly changed in order to protect the privacy of the people with whom I worked.

2. Frymer-Kensky argues that it wasn't until the 1st century BCE that sin was discussed as originating in paradise and not until the 1st century CE that Eve was blamed for it. See *In the Wake of the Goddesses: Women, Culture and the Biblical Transformation of Pagan Myth,* NY: Fawcett Columbine, 1992.

3. Genesis 1:26

4. R. Jeremiah b. Elazar, Genesis Rabbah 8:1; Brakhot 61a in Epstein, Rabbi I. (ed.), 1978, *The Babylonian Talmud, London: Soncino Press.;* R. Samuel b. Nachmani, Zohar I: 22b and 47a. in S.R. Ashlag, (comm..), R. Michaelberg (ed.) The Zohar, NY: Yeshivat Kol Yehuda.

5. When a word is emphasized, this repetition is a construct used in the Bible. It can mean "You will die die," or as Rabbi Ullman suggests, "In your dying, you shall die," (Genesis 2:17).

6. Genesis 2:18

7. This concept is expanded in Jean Baker Miller and Irene Stiver's book *The Healing Connection,* Boston: Beacon Press, 1997. Janet Surrey and Judith Jordan also developed the relational model discussed in this text. They underline the importance of mutual empathy and mutual authenticity and suggest that people suffer from isolation and grow in vital and energetic ways from strong, mutual connections.

8. There are a number of commentaries that take the position that Eve was created from Adam. For example, in Pirkei d'Rabbi Eliezer 12 (*The Babylonian Talmud*), it is written that God took a bone and flesh from Adam and made a helper. However, the word "tzele," which is often assumed to mean rib, is also used in the Hebrew Bible to mean the side of the ark. Also, creation in the Hebrew Bible is a separation process (light from dark, heavens

from earth, etc.) Therefore, it can also be understood that the two human beings were created through the separation of the male and female sides of the creature.

9. The next step of this idea can be found in Harriet Lerner's work *The Dance of Intimacy,* NY: Harper & Row, 1989. She writes that the women who changed how they participated in relationships were able to define a more whole and separate "I" that provided the groundwork for a more "intimate and gratifying 'we'." (p.3). While Adam could begin to define himself through a relationship with Eve, the more they know themselves (and themselves-in-relationship), the more intimate their relationship can become. That will happen later on, after they take a bite from the Tree of Knowledge.

10. From this point on, I will call the woman "Eve." However, in the Bible, she is not named Eve until after they leave the Garden of Eden.

11. It is even said that when Eve was created, Satan was also created! (Eitz Yosef 17:6, Warsaw, 1866/7). Eve is also blamed for causing Adam to die (Yerushalmi Shabbos 2:6, Hahary, T. trans. 1989. In *The Talmud of the land of Israel,* Chicago, IL: University of Chicago Press). However, not all traditional texts malign Eve. For example, when it is written in Psalms 1:6 that God recognizes the way of the righteous, the Shocher tov or Midrash on Psalms 1:10 (Yale Judaica Series Vol XII, New Haven, 1959) explains that this refers to Adam and Eve.

12. Quotations are rewritten using different words and are at times representative of a compilation of client voices that represent a theme in therapy. I do this to protect confidentiality.

13. Genesis 3:9,11.

14. Genesis 3:13

15. Deuteronomy 11:26

16. See also Rabbi Kushner's text, *How Good Do We Have to Be?*, Little, Brown & Co. 1996

17. Merle Feld wrote a very moving poem on this topic entitled "Yom Kippur Break." It can be found in her book *A Spiritual Life: A Jewish Feminist Journey,"* SUNY Press: Albany, 1999.

18. Kushner, *How Good Do We Have to Be?*, Little, Brown & Co. 1996

19. Arguing for male dominance, Josephus (Against Apion, ii, 24) writes: "Woman, says the Law, is in all things inferior to man. Let her accordingly be submissive, not for humiliation, but that she may be directed; for authority has been given by God to man." Judith Antonelli, in her text *In the Image of God: A Feminist Commentary on Torah,* N.J.: Jason Aronson,1995, points out that the word for "rule" in the Hebrew Bible does not have the same root as the word for "rule by domination" or "king," and implies instead "affinity or complementarity" (p. 13). She also points out that the Kabbalists believe that when we left Eden, we descended from a higher to a lower plane. Therefore, Antonelli argues, male supremacy is not ordained by God but instead demonstrates the imperfections of a world in exile.

20. Genesis 3:19

21. Genesis 3:20-21. "In the biblical text, the words sin and fall do not appear, but expel does occur. Expulsion is one phase of giving birth: the fetus is expelled from the mother's body where all that is necessary for life has been provided. It is after the expulsion that life begins-work, exertion, and sexuality." Solle, D. (1993), *Great Women of the Bible in Art and Literature,* quoted in *Talking About Genesis, a Resource Guide,* Public Affairs TV, Doubleday, NY: 1996, p43.

22. Barbara Grizzuti Harrison wrote a beautifully poetic essay on this theme in *Out of the Garden: Women Writers on the Bible,* edited by Christina Buchman and Celina Spiegel, NY: Fawcett Columbine, 1994.

SARAH, HAGAR AND ABRAHAM: EMPATHY AND BELONGING

CLAIRE AND JOHN *sat in my office, barely able to meet each other's gaze. Tearfully, Claire reported, "I just can't get John to listen to me. He's so insensitive. Last week, my dad called and told me everything I'm doing wrong in bringing up Lizzy. I was crying and I tried to get John to listen to me. I told him that I was hurt and mad and just wished I could tell my father off. After two seconds, John left to call my dad, and before I knew it, they were fighting. John just couldn't be there for me." John looked puzzled. For the world of him, he couldn't figure out why Claire was angry with him. Why couldn't Claire see his efforts to help? Why wasn't she grateful to have such a loving, loyal spouse? Defensive and angry, he seemed to pull further back in his chair. Claire sensed his subtle movement, and felt even more alone. "If only John would listen..." Her voice was barely audible. What was unsaid was that she wanted John to listen to her in a particular way. For Claire, and for many of us, listening means pausing long enough to enter the experience of the person we love. It means not giving advice or taking action, but simply being in the moment with that person. It is the hallmark of empathy, the quality we have when we resonate with the heart and soul of another. Deep listening and empathic relationships are gloriously difficult to develop and maintain, and gratefully, we can turn to the Hebrew Bible to learn about both the beauty of that empathic connection, and the cost of its denial.*

In the story of Sarah, Abraham and Hagar, one can understand God's role as demonstrating and instructing our foreparents about how to be in a meaningful relationship. Over and over again, God attempts to teach them—and us—that empathy is the core of loving relationships. Our foreparents stumble and they get it and they stumble again. And they give us a gift, because through their triumphs and mistakes, we too can learn how to be more empathic human beings committed more fully to our relationships.

So, let's enter a story that may teach us about developing empathic relationships, and the perils we encounter along the way. Our story begins in Genesis 12:1. Here we meet Avram,[1] whom we will later know as Abraham, an economically successful seventy-five-year-old man who resides in Haran, the land of his birth, with his wife and extended family. Hearing God's voice for the first time, Avram is told to leave his country and father's house, and according to some translations,[2] his kindred, and go to the land that God will show him. Avram immediately obeys, but in a way that gives us pause and makes us scratch our heads. He leaves Haran, but he takes with him his wife Sarai, his nephew Lot, and many members of his community. Is this any way to obey God? The Bible gives us a resounding "Yes!"

In United States dominant culture, we are told that to be truly mature, we need to go it alone. As parents, we are told to help our adolescents "separate and individuate." But, this is not the way of the Hebrew Bible. In many biblical stories,[3] living our lives means moving forward in life with those whom we love. It means recognizing the interdependence of all of us, and not only seeking autonomous achievement. If Avram is going to start a new life centered on God, then he will do it with those who help him along the path he must take.

Avram isn't alone in representing the relational values of Judaism. Moses felt that he couldn't return to Pharaoh and lead the Hebrews out of Egypt until God promised that his brother, Aaron, would accompany him. With the knowledge that Aaron would be there with him, that he didn't have to go it alone, Moses took on the challenge.[4] Much later, Naomi attempted to go back to Bethlehem alone, but her daughter-in-law Ruth was clear that they must face the future together.[5] This Holy Text encourages a religion of relationship. What a challenge for us as parents in the contemporary United States to encourage our children to stay connected, to resist the cultural imperative to lead autonomous lives. Yet, the prototype for this is right there in the Hebrew Bible. The challenge is to discover how to participate more fully in mutually caring and empathic relationships.

Avram and Sarai encounter their first relational dilemma when they reach Canaan, the Promised Land. Earlier,[6] God promised Avram, "To thy seed, I will give the land." There was no parallel promise made to Sarai. Here she is, an elderly, childless woman who leaves everything she knows to follow her husband and her God to a new life. Yet, now that she's in the Promised Land, she might not even be able to participate in this new life. After all, Sarai is seemingly too old to bear children. Avram could take a new, younger wife, one with whom he would more likely be able to fulfill God's promise of procreation. And then where would Sarai be? Far from home and all that is familiar, she might have no role in the life that is being created. And here we see her first error, and an error that she will struggle with again: She is silent. In the face of silence, there is no opportunity to work out the problem, and it can grow until it takes over our lives.

If I were Sarai, and if I knew my husband was expected to father a nation although I was past childbirth age, I would have reason to feel very anxious and worried about my future with him. At the same time, in all these years, Avram had stayed loyal to Sarai and had never taken another wife even though Sarai was childless. But things are about to get more uncertain, more frightening for Sarai. A famine ravishes Canaan, and Avram decides to take his family to Egypt, or Mitzrayim, in search of sustenance. The problem is that one just doesn't go to Mitzrayim if one wants sustenance. Mitzrayim comes from the root "narrow;"[7] it is a place where spirituality is closed off, where spiritual sustenance is absent. As if to underline the emptiness of Mitzrayim, God does not speak to Avram during the entire time he is there.

A moment for an aside: I use the word "Mitzrayim," and not the English translation "Egypt." Egypt is a physical space, a country complete with a beautiful culture and heritage. I would never insult that location and its people by calling it narrow. However, "Mitzrayim," the narrow place, needs no geographical boundaries. It is the place we find ourselves whenever we feel stuck. This is a land we're either too frightened to leave or always trying to leave, and one that we're always at risk of reentering. So, when my friend works long, long hours and misses so many important moments of his daughter's life, he knows he's in his Mitzrayim. Someone else might be in Mitzrayim because she feels stuck in a job for which she feels no passion, and yet she fears leaving the job security. We all have our Mitzrayims.

So what could be Avram's Mitzrayim? Avram tells Sarai that if Pharaoh sees how beautiful she is, he would kill Avram in order to marry Sarai. He therefore asks Sarai to pretend she's his sister. That way, Pharaoh could take her as a wife without risking Avram's life. Given Sarai's childlessness and God's promise to give the land to Avram's children, this plan could feel threatening to Sarai. After all, she is facing the possibility of a forced marriage. Worse, if Pharaoh takes her for a wife, she'd no longer be Avram's partner and he would be free to marry a woman who could bear children. The fact that we are never told that Avram emotionally resonated with the consequences for Sarai, the fact that there was no recorded discussion between them of the risks, is the empathic lapse on his part that defines his "Mitzrayim." Throughout his life, Avram will have to work to avoid these empathic lapses. Disconnected from his spiritual awareness (he didn't hear God while in Mitzrayim), and from his relational awareness of Sarai, Avram is stuck in a narrow place.

While some of our sages were upset with Avram's behavior, others tried to excuse it by saying that Sarai really was his half-sister.[8] But even if Avram is being honest about their familial relationship, he still doesn't take into account the suffering that Sarai could encounter as a result of his plan, so he is still stuck in a narrow place. When I taught this story to a third grade class, one of the children commented, "If Avram was so worried that Pharaoh would think Sarai was beautiful, they should have dressed her up as a bent-over ugly person." This eight-year-old thought of an alternative plan. He was not in a narrow place.

After taking Sarai for a wife, Pharaoh suffers from plagues and discovers that Sarai is Avram's wife. Pharaoh admonishes Avram for misleading him and tells him to leave Egypt, but Pharaoh, in awe of God, also rewards Avram with great wealth. Under those circumstances, it is hard for Avram to learn from his experience. After all, he is given gifts for his poor behavior! We all know that rewarding disturbing behavior encourages that behavior to reoccur, and so it will again. Later, Avram again passes Sarai off as his sister when he feels endangered by another king, and again God intervenes on Sarai's behalf.[9]

It is disturbing that when Pharoah frees Sarai, Avram does

not respond. There is no mention in the Bible of Avram and Sarai's reunion. There is no mention of his apologizing, crying with remorse and relief when he sees her, or hugging her close and reassuring her that this will not happen again. Only silence. For the second time, a problem emerges and is met with silence instead of discussion and healing.

The next time we meet Sarai she is a more proactive, vibrant actor than she had been up until this point. Still childless, still committed to the covenant God made with Avram, she now also has the knowledge that Avram would leave her and allow her to marry another man if he thought it were necessary. What could she do? If she did nothing, she could end up without a husband or family or future. She couldn't wait and let the next crisis lead him to abandon her to the next Pharaoh. Worse, possibly, was that if she didn't take action, Avram might not be able to fulfill the covenant. Sarai was deeply committed to God and the covenant, yet each year it became less likely that the covenant would be fulfilled. Unless. Unless Sarai stopped waiting and took some action both to secure her own future and to secure God's promise to Avram. What could this elderly woman possibly do? It is at this point that I imagine Sarai having the creative and problematic thought that would turn everything on its head. Sarai thinks of Hagar, her Egyptian maidservant. Hagar literally means "the stranger." Hagar, the stranger, could help Sarai not become the stranger herself. Hagar could have Avram's baby for Sarai. Through this stranger, Sarai could once again feel a sense of belonging. Perhaps at that moment Sarai feels abandoned by God, who after all has no covenant with her, and by Avram, who already had given her to Pharaoh. In a last, desperate, effort she tries to make herself belong. Or, perhaps Sarai feels a responsibility to activate the process of making God's covenant a reality. Either way, Hagar could be her vehicle. And that's the problem, that is what becomes Sarai's Mitzrayim: when another person becomes our vehicle, that person loses her humanity in our eyes, and we enter the role of oppressor.

Perhaps Sarai even tries to involve Hagar as ethically as possible. For example, Sarai suggests that Avram marry her Egyptian handmaid, not that Hagar merely sexually service Avram.[10] But, nowhere in this passage does Sarai empathetically connect with Hagar. Nowhere does she wonder what it must be like for Hagar to become pregnant and carry a baby that she'll never be permitted to influence as a mother or raise as an Egyptian. In one fell swoop, Hagar's maternity and her ethnicity will be traded for Sarai's, and Hagar will simply be a handmaiden with more status than other servants.

After Hagar becomes pregnant, Sarai complains to her husband that Hagar despises her. Sarai assumes that Hagar's change in attitude is because Sarai is infertile while Hagar so easily conceived. The maid moved into the one up position, and Sarai is left feeling inferior even to her servant. Sarai's feelings are understandable.

A forty-year-old patient said to me, "I've been trying to get pregnant for twelve years. No fertility treatment has helped. Everytime I see a pregnant woman, I want to cry. I feel that she's superior to me, that she's the complete woman and I'm defective. I know it's not logical, and I'm a chemist and I'm trained to think logically. But it's about my feelings. I just don't feel whole compared to women who conceive."

Because of that heightened vulnerability, Sarai does not consider that Hagar could despise her for reasons other than Sarai's infertility. While the Hebrew Bible teaches us to love and not do anything to hurt the stranger,[11] this stranger, Hagar, is placed in the very difficult situation of serving Sarai and bearing a child for her. Sarai does not understand the feelings that might be growing in Hagar along with this child: the love for the yet-to-be-born baby, the hopes and dreams that will never be fulfilled because the baby will be taken from her to be raised by Sarai. Perhaps Hagar does not despise Sarai for her childlessness, but rather for the way Sarai responds to her childlessness.

It is at those moments of self-involvement that we need our loved ones to be there for us, supporting us and listening to our burdens, and offering us the opportunity to enlarge our perspective. Perhaps regretting that she had ever suggested that Avram marry Hagar, Sarai angrily says to her husband "My wrong be upon thee ....."[12] Here we once again experience Avram's empathic lapse. He does not reassure her that no woman and no other woman's child will ever diminish his love for Sarai or undermine her position as his first wife and love. He doesn't try to work out the misunderstandings between the vulnerable Sarai and her opressed servant. At the time when we're feeling most upset, most hurt, we turn to the ones we love for comfort and support. Sarai turns to Avram, but Avram does not lend her an attentive ear or emotional comfort. Avram's response is "Behold, thy maid is in thy hand; do to her as it pleases thee." With nobody to understand her, and her self-involvement causing her to lose her own relational compass, Sarai takes out her hurt and bitterness abusively on her hapless servant.[13]

What a statement to make in a sacred text! Sarai, our revered foremother, a woman of deep spirituality and great kindness, can be abusive. What a cautionary message for all of us. If Sarai can become abusive, so can we. The potential for good and for evil is in each of us, and the Hebrew Bible does not try to hide that truth from us.

How many times I've seen the Sarai-Avram-Hagar scenario played out in my office! A young mother is overwhelmed by her three preschoolers. She tells her husband that she's exhausted and the kids don't listen and she can't stand how they're behaving. Her husband says, "What am I supposed to do? I'm working all day. You're their mother. You deal with it." Next thing we know, a child is beaten. I'm not writing this to excuse the abusive parent—she has the moral responsibility to refrain from abuse no matter how upset she is. But, I am saying that we can sometimes prevent abuse by empathically listening to and supporting our friends and partners.

This isn't only about physical abuse. When we're having a hard time and there's nobody there to support us, we're more likely to be irritable and thoughtless toward our loved ones, to say something that hurts instead of something that's understanding, or to lash out at something small that we could otherwise deal with constructively. If we feel empty and we can't get replenished, we have nothing left to give to those who need us. Empathy is the replenishing water, and empathy had yet to be developed in Avram and Sarai.

Tragically, Sarai becomes abusive to Hagar, and Hagar runs away "bamidbar," into the wilderness. Bamidbar comes from the word "daber," or speak.[14] How can the wilderness be a place of speech when what we're often struck by is its silence? Who speaks to us in a place so devoid of other people? As Hagar soon finds out, the wilderness is the place we enter when we need to hear God speak to us. It is that place deep inside us that can feel so lonely and yet, if we enter that space and listen, we can hear and feel in a way that can completely alter our lives. Life is never the same again after we journey into the wilderness, so it is often with fear and trepidation that we take those steps.

One of my colleagues had been a lawyer for years. She was financially secure and well respected in her field, but she felt personally lost. When she took the time and had the courage to enter her wilderness, she heard clearly that this was no longer the right place for her to be, that she had to journey to a more meaningful place. She had always wanted to be a teacher, and although it scared her to change her job so dramatically, she recognized that she had to start paying attention to the quiet but persistent voice, the voice she heard in her wilderness.

So, a scared Hagar runs away to the wilderness, and a messenger of God speaks to her. How remarkable! In a text holy to the Jewish people, the first time a messenger of God speaks to a woman, who is chosen? A non-Hebrew, an Egyptian, someone who will become the mother of another religion! As remarkable, God, who could chose to speak to anyone, choses a poor servant, a woman of color, a person who was marginalized in her society then and would be marginalized in ours today. The God of this particular story does not discriminate based on race, class, gender, or ethnicity. Whoever we are and however we are treated by our society, if we are willing to listen, we can hear God in the deepest recesses of our hearts and souls.

Interestingly, the messenger meets Hagar on her way to Shur, meaning "look or envision." What is Hagar looking for? Perhaps she is trying to envision freedom, but has not yet arrived there. The Hebrew Bible tells us that when the messenger asks Hagar who she is and where she was going, she says that she is running away from her mistress Sarai. She has not yet envisioned what she is running toward, nor can she envision herself as Hagar, a woman not defined by her servitude to Sarai.

31

When my colleague first became disenchanted with her law career, she complained a lot about the ethics, hours, and belief system of the firm. But, when people met her and asked her about herself, she replied that she was a lawyer. At that point, she didn't know where she was heading or how to define herself as other-than-lawyer. Until she had that new vision, she couldn't leave her firm and become a teacher. She remained identified as a lawyer until she developed her new vision.

Hagar has the same experience. When she could not tell the angel where she is going, or who she is separate from her servitude toward Sarai, the messenger tells her to return to Sarai. This could be a harsh message, but the messenger delivers it with empathy. Hagar is told that she will have many descendents. She will give birth to a son named "Ishmael," which means "God heard," because God heard Hagar's affliction.

Years later, God will again hear affliction, but this time it will be that of the Hebrews at the hands of the Egyptians. Again, this will be followed by the birth of a special child. Again, God will be with us in the wilderness and show us the way. After our foreparents behaved so unempathically to Hagar, perhaps we needed to experience firsthand what the stranger experienced so that we can access that memory when we are tempted to once again dehumanize other human beings.[15]

Hagar is also told that Ishmael will be "a wild ass of a man, his hand will be against every man and every man's hand against him; and he shall dwell in the presence of all his brethren." At first, this sounds like a curse more than a blessing. However, there are several ways to understand this statement as a blessing that God bestows upon Hagar. First, the word for "wild ass," or "pereh," is also used in Jacob's blessing to Joseph, indicating that this is indeed a blessing given by God to Hagar. At that time, a wild ass was seen as a beautiful animal that could never be domesticated. I remembered a conversation I had years ago with a Holocaust survivor. She told me that several years after she was liberated from the camps, she gave birth to a son. She wished that he would grow into a powerful man, one who could fight anyone who tried to harm him and would be strong enough never to be hurt or forced to leave again. For someone with this mother's experience, that son would be a blessing. To a disempowered, abused Hagar, God offered hope and a future through Ishmael.

A close look at the Hebrew shows us that God's words about Ishmael can also be translated as Ishmael's hand will be "in" rather than "against" every man's hand and he will live in sight of his brothers. For Hagar the outsider, the stranger, this can be a blessing. While she is separated from all that she knows and loves, her son will grow up with what is familiar: He might be wild but he will be connected; he will never suffer exile.

Hagar understands God's words as a blessing, and her response is to be the first woman in the Hebrew Bible to name God. She names God "Thou God seest me."[16] From Hagar's response, we are instructed for all eternity what is involved in true empathy. God demonstrates empathy by seeing Hagar (as she notes when she names God) and by hearing Hagar (as noted in Ishmael's name). Empathy involves seeing the other—not rendering the other invisible because of ethnicity, gender, race or class. It involves hearing the other and responding to what you hear. God sees Hagar and God hears her, and for this, Hagar is grateful.

While empathy by itself is wonderful, empathy is not enough. Mutual empathy completes this picture. Mutual empathy is when we recognize and resonate with another's empathy toward us. After Hagar feels heard and seen by God, she wonders, "Have I also here looked after the one who sees me?"[17] In response she names a well, Be'er-lahay-ro'i, meaning, "The well of the Life that sees me." Hagar resonates with God's empathic response to her. She shows God that she feels the Eternal's empathy by her own empathic naming of the well in God's honor.

Interestingly, the well is located between Quadesh and Bered, between the holy and the plague of hail. Journeying between blessing and plague, where she wishes to be and where she has been, Hagar made her peace with God. A changed Hagar returns to Sarai and Avram. This Hagar has experienced the empathy of being heard and seen by God. She knows she will have a son and that there is hope in the future. And she knows that she is close to having a vision of freedom.

Immediately after she names the well, we are told that Hagar gives birth to a son, and Avram "called his son's name, whom Hagar bore, Yishmael."[18] Hagar's wilderness transformation goes beyond Hagar and touches the entire family. We don't hear that Hagar bears Avram and Sarai a son. We never hear Sarai's named mentioned in relationship to this baby. We do hear twice that Hagar is the mother of this child. We never hear Hagar referred to as a servant in this verse. And, we hear Ishmael called not simply Hagar's child, but Avram's son. So, Hagar never does give her child over to Sarai, nor do we ever hear of Sarai abusing Hagar after her return from the wilderness. Instead, we hear of Ishmael as the acknowledged son of Avram and Hagar. God truly did see and hear this stranger.

Then the Hebrew Bible is silent about the next thirteen years. In the time it takes Ishmael to reach what is now understood as the age of Bar Mitzvah, in the time it takes for him to develop into a young man, we hear nothing. Yet, at the end of these thirteen years God again appears to Avram with the name "El Shaddai."

While this is often translated as "God Almighty," Shaddai also comes from the root meaning "breast." It is the God who is the breast who now appears to Avram--the God who will reveal God-self as ready to deliver nurturance and teach it to others. If any form of the Eternal can teach about empathy, it is El Shaddai, the God of Nurturance. And this God forms a covenant with Avram, changes his name to Abraham and Sarai's to Sarah, and tells Abraham that he will have a son with Sarah.

First, Abraham laughs with joy and wonderment that he and Sarah are to become parents in their old age. Then, in one of the most beautifully empathic verses in this story, Abraham responds, "O that Ishmael might live before thee!"[19] Abraham is worried about the future of his known child. What will happen to his beloved son if his new son is chosen to fulfill the covenant? At that moment, Abraham might choose not to have another child rather than cause suffering to the child he knows and loves. El Shaddai acknowledges Abraham's empathic outcry. God tells Abraham that although the covenant is with Isaac, both of his sons will father great nations. God promises that Ishmael will be the father of princes, while Isaac will carry on the covenant.

Even before Sue's daughter was born, she was excited about teaching her how to play the piano. By the time Jamie was five years old, she was already taking lessons and playing duets with her mom. The problem was that Jamie didn't like the piano. She had neither the easy talent that allows some children to learn with very little practice, nor the desire for the hard earned talent that requires a great deal of practicing. Lethargically, she would chop out the duets, and Sue's heart grew heavier and heavier. Finally, Sue had to recognize that even though she cried, "Oh, that Jamie might play the piano," Jamie would never be a pianist. The blessing was allowing

Jamie to stop and become the dreamer of her own dream, the leader of her own nation. Perhaps none of Sue's children will play the piano, but perhaps her infant son Brian will have the passion and that covenant will be with him. One of the hardest jobs of parenting is recognizing which, if any, of our children will be the ones to carry on our strongest passions, our covenant, and how to recognize that our children have to become the parents of their own nations. Gently, God teaches Abraham how to be the parent who allows Ishmael to become the father of princes and allows Isaac to carry on the covenant.

Shortly after this conversation with God, Sarah becomes pregnant and gives birth to Isaac, or "laughter." When Isaac is weaned, his father makes a huge feast. At the feast, Sarah sees Ishmael laughing, and responds by telling Abraham that Isaac will not share Abraham's inheritance with Ishmael, and that Abraham must cast out Hagar and Ishmael. Many of our rabbis, troubled by Sarah's powerful response, sought to interpret Ishmael's behavior. Perhaps he was mocking Isaac, and Sarah could no longer tolerate Isaac's hurt. Perhaps he was even abusive. Yet, other commentators argue that there is no linguistic reason to believe that Sarah saw anything except Ishmael laughing or playing.[20] Why, then, would Sarah be so upset?

Anybody who has experienced jealousy and insecurity knows the answer to that question. Imagine Abraham, an elderly man who has grown to love his now fifteen-year-old son, Ishmael, over the many years they shared together. Now imagine a two-year-old toddler. Perhaps Sarah is worried that Abraham is not as connected to her Isaac as he is to Hagar's Ishmael. He wouldn't be the first father to find it easier to connect with a teenager than with a baby in diapers. Would the covenant be with Ishmael? Or, just as bad, would Isaac grow up in Ishmael's shadow? And, Ishmael is laughing! "Laughter" is Isaac's name. Could this mean that Ishmael is taking over Isaac's position, claiming rights as the firstborn son?

Sarah might wonder if she could trust Abraham to truly love and honor her son. After all, he did risk her life twice by passing her off as his sister to the kings of foreign countries, and he didn't take an actively empathic role when she had problems with Hagar. Her fears and insecurities building, she tells Abraham to get rid of the people whom she perceives as her rivals and her son's rivals.

Sarah's demand to Abraham is actually a more familiar scenario than we might initially imagine. Soon after his new sister arrived home from the hospital, three-year-old Josh said, "Take her back. Let's go back to the hospital with Becky." We can assume that Josh felt threatened by this intruder who was taking so much of his parents' time and getting so much of everyone's attention. He might have felt left out and unwanted. However, it is unlikely that his parents would say, "Okay, let's pack her up and off we go!" Instead, Josh's parents would probably reassure Josh of how much he is loved, needed and part of their expanding family. But who is there to reassure Sarah when her insecurities lead to another empathic lapse?

We don't even know for certain what Sarah means when she says to Abraham, "Cast out this bondwoman and her son for the son of this bondwoman shall not be heir with my son."[21] Does she want him to send the child and his mother into the wilderness? Or is she asking him to cast them out of his thoughts so that they won't compete with Isaac for the inheritance? We find out how Abraham understands the request but we have no idea what Sarah tries to communicate. One of the liabilities of silence in a relationship is that we don't check out what the other means, and we act based solely on our own interpretation.

God recognizes Abraham's distress as he contemplates sending his beloved older son and his second wife into the wilderness, and God tries to instruct Abraham about being a reassuring, empathic spouse: "In all that Sarah has said to thee, 'shma b'kola,' listen to or listen in, her voice. For in Isaac shall thy seed be called, and also of the son of the bondwoman will I make a nation..."[22] The heart of this entire story lies in how we understand the phrase "listen to her voice." *Josh's parents could have listened to Josh by obeying him and taking Becky back to the hospital. But, Josh's parents could also listen by empathically hearing not simply his words, but also the cadence of his voice. While words communicate language, voice communicates feeling. By listening to Josh's voice, his parents could hear his pain and fear, and they could hold him and reassure him of their love and of how much they want and need him in the family.*

Perhaps God is trying to teach Abraham how to "hear into" the voice of a loved one, how to experience empathic love. God might be telling Abraham to listen to, meaning be with and hear, Sarah. And perhaps God is telling Abraham to pay attention to her voice, to the meaning behind the words. If Abraham could listen to Sarah's voice, he would be able to hear Sarah's insecurities and her fears. Then, using the divinely inspired words, Abraham could reassure her that there is no cause for alarm because God will make great nations of both the boys. But Abraham does not understand God's words in this way. Instead of stopping to listen, he moves to act.

How excruciatingly and brilliantly human to discover that the same problems we face today confronted our foreparents thousands of years ago. I was working with a couple, Nora and Jeff. Nora had broken her ankle and was hospitalized because of complications. She told Jeff that she needed him because she was in a lot of pain. Jeff, a physician, responded by calling a number of the most experienced doctors for con-sultations. He was hurt, angry and confused when Nora told Jeff that he had let her down and that she was upset with him. What had Jeff done?

He fell into the same trap as Abraham. When he heard the word "need," he assumed Nora meant that Jeff should do something, and a well-meaning Jeff went into action mode to get the consultations. When God said "listen" to Sarah's voice, Abraham thought God meant obey and went into action mode by expelling Hagar and Ishmael. But, as I tell many of the het-erosexual couples with whom I work, "Men might believe in the statement 'don't just sit there, do something;' but women often need you to 'don't just do something, sit there'!" Nora wanted Jeff to sit with her and comfort her. His empathic presence would help allay her fears and contain her anxiety. Instead, he unwittingly lost that moment by taking action. At the start of this chapter, Claire was angry with John for the same reason--she needed her husband to be with her emo-tionally rather than to run off to solve the problem. Similarly, Sarah might have needed Abraham to sit with her through her fears, to comfort and reassure her, but in an effort to be helpful, Abraham might have lost that moment by taking action.

And action was taken. We are told that Abraham rises early in the morning, takes bread and a bottle of water and gives it to Hagar. He then sends her and Ishmael away into the wilderness. Where is Sarah? We don't know. We never hear another word from her after she asks Abraham to send Hagar away. We don't hear from her on the morning of their departure, nor do we hear from her the morning her own son leaves with Abraham on their journey to bind and sacrifice Isaac on Mt. Moriah. The seed of silence in the face of adversity that was sown early in this story now grows wildly and silences all possibility for reconciliation. The next time Sarah is mentioned is when we are informed of her death--but no final words come from her mouth, and our questions about her remain unanswered.

At least they are unanswered in the Hebrew Bible, but through our own Midrash and those of the Jewish sages, we can read between the black letters and into the white spaces and we can give her words. I can only imagine what it must have felt to Sarah to wake up that morning and find that her servant of so many years and the child whom she wanted to raise as her son are both gone. Worse, they are gone because of some angry, inflammatory words that she had uttered to her husband. And not only are they gone, but they might be dead. Abraham had given them only one bottle of water, and the wilderness is a big, empty space. How could she ever trust herself to speak again, believing that her words were responsible for the pain and possible death of two people who were her rivals but with whom she also had an intense relationship? After all, isn't Sarah also "hagar," the stranger? Didn't she, too, feel like a stranger when she was unable to conceive in a marriage that relied on conception to fulfill the covenant? Didn't she also feel like an outsider when her husband showed his love for Ishmael and she worried that Isaac would not find a place with his father? Didn't she feel like a second-class servant when the women around her conceived but she was barren? Don't we often struggle most with the people who remind us most of ourselves? Sarah loses a part of herself when Hagar is cast out, and perhaps she feels that lest she do any more harm, she needs to be silent.

In the Hebrew Bible, though, silence is not the avenue for solving problems, for repentance or for movement in life. Silence is a disconnection—it does not allow for repairing relationships. We are told that when Sarah died, "Sarah was one hundred and twenty-seven years old: These were the years of Sarah's life."[23] We don't hear that she died "full of years" like Abraham. I can almost feel Sarah's emptiness and sorrow, dying in Qiryat-arba alone while her husband is living in Beersheva.

Twelve years ago, my mother-in-law was dying of cancer. Even as she weakened physically, her spirit seemed to grow stronger. She welcomed all visitors with an acceptance that made them know that she loved them and forgave them for any issues that might have come up in their lives together. Her son, daughter-in-law, grandchildren and beloved friend surrounded her during the last day of her life. Although we miss her terribly, we are comforted that she died peacefully, surrounded by both the love she emanated and the love we all felt for her. I wish Sarah could have had that experience. But, with her silence and isolation, she couldn't reach out to Hagar, Ishmael, Abraham, Isaac and any others she might have loved, wronged and been wronged by. Perhaps we, now, can remember Sarah with love and understanding, and learn from her so that we can live more connected, relationally full lives.[24]

But what of Hagar and Ishmael? We left them turned out by Abraham, with pitifully little food and water. For the second time, Hagar enters the wilderness, the place where one speaks with God. This time, though, perhaps she has a vision. She has a son with Abraham. Her status has been elevated. In spite of Sarah's initial assumption that she would raise Ishmael, Hagar is both the biological and spiritual mother of Ishmael. That sense of herself as some-

41

thing more than simply Sarah's bondwoman changes her from the insecure maid who ran away years earlier. This time, she enters the wilderness perhaps frightened, but also with a vision of a God with whom she communicates, and of a son who will be a ruler of nations.

But, the water is used up, probably both physically and spiritually. Perhaps she couldn't sustain her vision through the hard wilderness journey. Without that faith, that spiritual sustenance, how could she have any hope of making it through the wilderness? So, Hagar places her dying child under a shrub and leaves him there. She can't bear to see her child die. As understandable as her anguish is, her empathic lapse looms large. When a child is in pain and dying, what he needs most is the loving embrace of his parent. To leave him at that moment is so self-protective and so lacking in compassion that God intervenes and hears Ishmael's voice, the voice from which Hagar has tried to distance.

We all know and have been Hagars at the moment she distanced from Ishmael. I remember hearing a childhood neighbor yelling at her son, "Stop crying before I give you something to cry about!" The words, however illogical, are familiar--most of us have either been that parent, that child, or that neighbor. What would prompt that mother to say those words? Sometimes, it is our own discomfort with the pain of others that leads us to treat them unempathically. By cutting off our empathic feelings that resonate with their pain, we protect ourselves from feeling their pain. But, we do so at the expense of our relationship with the other person. The Hebrew Bible is clear that when our self-protective response is to disengage from a loved one who needs us, our responsibility is to empathically reconnect with that person. Only then can the person we love and we begin the healing journey.

In a poignant verse, God teaches Hagar what she needs to do to regain her empathy. God tells Hagar, "Arise, lift up the lad, and hold him in thy hand."[25] Hagar needs to offer Ishmael comfort and support during this desperate time. One's own pain is no excuse for ignoring the suffering of another, especially that of a child. And, as Hagar holds her son, regains her empathy and her compassion and is able to comfort the child, God opens her eyes and she sees a well of water. Through connection to others, through allowing ourselves to reach beyond ourselves to empathically hold another, we can find the sustenance and salvation that have been available to us all along.[26]

In the Hebrew Bible, water often is a metaphor for spiritual sustenance. When Hagar is emotionally available to her son, she is once again open to receiving spiritual sustenance. She maintains her empathy as she fills the bottle with water and offers it first to Ishmael before drinking any herself. She thus offers Ishmael both the physical and spiritual nourishment he needs to make this journey.

We are told that God is with Ishmael, and he grows up in the wilderness in Paran. Paran may mean ash or pine tree, and trees provide shelter from the burning sun. Even though Ishmael grows up in the wilderness, he may be sheltered from hardship, the metaphoric burning sun, because God is with him. Hagar's story ends when we are told she finds an Egyptian wife for Ishmael.[27] Not only is she the only woman in the Bible to find a wife for her son, but this is the final indication that her ethnicity, not Sarah's, is passed on to Ishmael.

This passage is clear that God is with Hagar and Ishmael even though they are not Hebrews. Hagar, a stranger, who is not a member of the dominant culture ethnically or racially, who is not wealthy, and who is female, has two encounters with the God of

43

Israel, and feels seen and heard by that God. In this particular story, the God we worship is empathic with all human creation, not differentiating based on race, class, ethnicity, or gender. God is also present for Sarah, as the Eternal instructs Abraham that empathy is an act of deep, committed listening. Abraham also feels God's empathy, as he is reassured during a moment of grief that both of his sons will become great nations. Hebrew and non-Hebrew, man and woman, poor and rich, all experience God's empathy when we are willing to stop and listen. And God, the ever-patient teacher, over and over demonstrates the power of empathy, the ingredients of empathy, the rewards of empathy, to those of us made in God's image but who too easily forget.

Notes

1. Abraham was called "Avram" and Sarah was named "Sarai" until God changed their names in Genesis 17:5 and 17:15.
2. In the Bible, ideas are not repeated within a sentence. So, if Avram is told to leave his birthplace and his native land, some translators (see, for example, *The Holy Scriptures, Masoretic Text,* Sinai Publishing, Israel.) say that this must have two meanings, and translate it as leaving both his native land and his kindred.
3. See, for example, Ruth and Naomi, Moses and Aaron, Barak and Deborah.
4. See Exodus 4:13-18.
5. See Ruth 1:15-16.
6. Genesis 12:7
7. Rabbi Alan Ullman taught me the metaphor of Egypt as a narrow place internally, not simply geographically.
8. Avram and Sarai were half-siblings, born of the same father and different mothers, so technically Avram was not lying when he told Pharaoh that Sarai was his sister. The Zohar 1:82a excuses Abraham's actions in Egypt saying

that Abraham had faith that God would not allow Sarah to be harmed and therefore did not believe he was putting her at risk. Nachmanides, on the other hand, considers Abraham's behavior to be sinful. The Plaut Commentary (UAHC, 1981, p. 100) states that "Jewish teaching has generally held that, even under duress, no man may intentionally kill or commit a sexual crime on an innocent person...Since both Sarah and Pharaoh were put in jeopardy by Abraham, the proper judgment would seem to support Nachmanides' comment: 'It was a sin.'" See C.B. Chavel, Ed. (1971), *Ramban/ Nachmanides Commentary on the Torah.* NY: Shiloh Publishing House, Inc.

9. See Genesis 20:2.

10. Genesis 16:3; Genesis Rabbah 45:3.

11. See, for example, Leviticus 19:33-34: "And if a stranger sojourn with thee in your land, you shall not wrong him. But the stranger that dwells with you shall be to you as one born among you, and thou shalt love him as thyself..." (Koren Publishers Translation, 1992)

12. Genesis 16:5. Some rabbis were critical of Avram's lack of responsiveness to Sarai when she confronted him about Hagar. Some commentaries envision Sarai criticizing Avram for never having prayed for a child on her behalf. Further, the commentators envision Sarai confronting Avram on his lack of responsiveness which she sees as depriving her of his words See Rashi from the *Saperstein Edition of the Torah: With Rashi's Commentary,* Rabbi Yisrael Isser Ziv Herezeg, et.al (Eds), Brooklyn, NY: Mesorah Publications Ltd. 1997; Genesis Rabbah 45:5

13. Genesis Rabbah (45:6) comments that Sarai restrained Hagar from sexual involvement with Avram, made her carry heavy buckets, and slapped her with a slipper. Nachmanides believed that both Avram and Sarai wronged Hagar.

14. Rabbi Alan Ullman pointed out that the root dbr (speak) is in midbar (wilderness).

15. Rabbi Daniel Hartman, in a talk at Temple Beth Elohim, Wellesley, discussed the empathy that can grow from the actual experience of being slaves in Egypt and the daily reminders of that experience that are included in our prayers. In Leviticus 19:34, we are reminded to love the stranger *because* we

were once strangers in the land of Egypt. The experience offers us a visceral reminder of how God wants us to behave.

16. Genesis 16:13.

17. Genesis 16:13

18. Genesis 16:15

19. Genesis 17:18

20. Commentators have read many different meanings into the line that Ishmael was playing/laughing with Isaac. One assumption is that Ishmael pretended to be playing as he shot an arrow at Isaac with the intent of killing him (Sefer haYashar P. 69, see Kornfeld, N.Y. & Walzer, A.B., NJ: KTAV publishing House, 1993). Rashi writes that Ishmael is also said to have boasted that he will take a double portion of the inheritance since he is the first born. Ishmael has also been accused of hunting and violating married women (Genesis Rabbah 53:11). E. Speiser, in the Anchor Bible Genesis, N.Y.: Doubleday & Co, 1964, responds that in order for the Hebrew word "mitzachek" to mean "mocking," a "b" prefix would be needed which is not present. He argues that there is nothing in the original Hebrew to support the idea that Ishmael was doing anything more than amusing Isaac.

21. Genesis 21:10

22. Genesis 21:12

23. Genesis 23:1

24. Jean Baker Miller and Irene Stiver, in their 1998 book *The Healing Connection,* discuss the pain of isolation and the process of moving from disconnection back into connection.

25. Genesis 21:18

26. Norman Cohen states "The beginning of Hagar's own salvation was her ability to reach out to Ishmael and give him the support he needed to survive" (*Self, Struggle and Change: Family Conflict Stories in Genesis and Their Healing Insights for Our Lives,* Woodstock, Vt.: Jewish Lights, 1995, p.78.) Similarly a premise in the mental health field is that when we move beyond our self-absorption and begin to reach out to others, we have entered onto the path of healing.

27. Some rabbis argue that this is not the end of Hagar's story. After the death of Sarah, Abraham married a woman named Keturah. According to Genesis Rabbah (61:4) as well as the Zohar (1:133b), Keturah was another name for Hagar, and thus Abraham and Hagar reconciled.

❈ 3 ❈

REBECCA: ENVISIONING OUR RELATIONSHIPS

WHEN I FIRST met sixteen-year-old Nicole, her silence screamed into every corner of my office. Slowly, words began to grope their way into small spaces, and one day, Nicole was even able to look at me with soft blue eyes that I had never before seen because her head had always been lowered, her eyes always focused on the floor. Nicole and I met daily in my office next to the psychiatric hospital ward on which she briefly resided. One day, during a halting discussion about the positive aspects of some of her relationships, I mentioned her frequent trips with her mother over the past two years to Shakespearean productions. Nicole's mom, a Shakespearean actress in local theater companies and a student of the Bard, would share ideas about the plays and express her desire to listen avidly to Nicole's perspective—a perspective rarely offered. On this particular day, when I mentioned the trips to the theatre, Nicole smiled vaguely and told me in a barely audible voice, "I don't like Shakespeare!" I was stunned. How could this be? How could she spend two years seemingly enthralled with Shakespearean plays, spending almost all her free afternoons attending performances, and not like Shakespeare?

As we talked, it became clear that Lara, Nicole's older sister who was now a college student, shared a deep interest in the playwright with their mother. Nicole too longed for a close and engaging relationship with her mother, but she didn't know how to connect with her authentically, as Nicole. Instead, she waited for Lara to leave for college, and then, in a sense, pretended to be her sister by passing herself off as interested in Shakespeare when in fact she didn't have the slightest interest in the subject. "So why not present yourself to your mom as Nicole?" I wondered aloud. Voice quivering, Nicole replied, "She wouldn't like the real Nicole."

As I listened to Nicole, I couldn't help but think of Rebecca, our visionary yet flawed biblical foremother, the foremother who could look into the heart and soul of those she loves and see them without pretense. How could I help thinking of Rebecca? After all, her son and her husband confronted the same situation as Nicole and her mom. Perhaps if I could learn from Rebecca, I could be of help to them.

To do this, I needed to begin by returning to Genesis 24, to a time before Rebecca entered our lives. Here we find out that Abraham was seeking a wife for his son, Isaac. I can only imagine what life must have felt like to Isaac at that moment. Thinking it was God's will, Abraham had taken Isaac up to the top of Mt. Mariah, bound him, and raised his knife to kill him before an angel stopped Abraham and a ram was substituted for the boy. Isaac and his father left the mountain separately, never to speak with each other again. The next thing we hear, Isaac's beloved mother had died. There are no words in the Torah indicating that Isaac and his mother were ever reunited after he returned from the mountain. Isaac's beloved mother, Sarah, had died before she could soothe him, before she could help him heal from the terrible trauma of near-death at the hands of his father. In mourning, Isaac had to deal with the loss of both his parents; with betrayal and distrust; with faith; and with his abject loneliness.

Abraham, however, may have learned something when

God's angel told him to stop the action at the altar. Abraham had been a man of action, but at that moment, he finally could stop long enough to truly listen with his heart and conscience and thus hear the messenger implore him to let his son live. By stopping and listening, Abraham experienced what it is like to be an empathic human being. The experience of empathy is expansive and enables one to enter relationships more fully. Instead of sacrificing his son, Abraham found a ram, a male parent of a lamb, tangled in the brush and sacrificed that ram. By sacrificing the entangled father-of-the-lamb, the part of himself that was caught up and bound,[1] he might have learned something critical about being able to hear and resonate with those whom he loved. We can hope that Abraham might then have been able to understand what so many of us do not: we hurt our children when we sacrifice them for any ideal, and if we listen to our innermost voice, that voice that some of us understand as God, we can stop sacrificing our children.

After Abraham sacrificed the ram, God informed Abraham that because Abraham did not withhold his son from God, God would bless Abraham.[2] Because Abraham listened to God's messenger and allowed Isaac to live, the covenant could be passed on through Isaac as had been intended by God. Stopping the action ended up allowing the larger action to unfold. Possibly as part of an effort to be a more untangled and caring father, Abraham decides to seek a wife for Isaac before he tries to find a new wife for himself.

Abraham sends his trusted servant Eliezar[3] to Haram Naharayim in search of a wife for Isaac. This is the land of Abraham's father and God had already told Abraham to leave that land in order to make a spiritual connection with God. This land remains a land of idol worshippers, a people who could be understood as worshipping what is meaningless and forgetting what has meaning. Abraham refuses to let Isaac enter that land. Perhaps Abraham wonders if Isaac would ever return to fulfill the covenant: Without his mother or a relationship with his father, Isaac might have been tempted to stay in Haram Naharayim and never return to the Promised Land. Or, perhaps Abraham recognizes that Isaac is no more than a shell of a man who had been too traumatized by the binding on Mt. Moriah to initiate a relationship on his own, so Isaac would not be able to find a wife if he were sent on that journey. In any case, Abraham sends Eliezar to Haram Naharayim, or Haran.

But Eliezar is worried about his task. Maybe the woman he finds will not want to return with him. How can he vow to bring home an unwilling wife for Isaac? Abraham, in a revolutionary statement acknowledging the humanity of women, tells Eliezar that he is only responsible for bringing back a wife for Isaac if the woman comes willingly. This is not to be a forced marriage. The choice is to be placed in her hands.

So, Eliezar sets out on his journey. Upon arriving at the well in Haran, Eliezer begs God to show "chesed," lovingkindness , to Abraham. Eliezar is very specific about what kind of woman would demonstrate God's chesed. Eliezar asks for a generous woman; a woman who not only would give him a drink, but also water his camels (Gen. 24:14). He does not ask for a woman of beauty. He does not ask for a virgin. He does not ask for any of the qualities that men traditionally sought in a bride. It is the inner qualities, not the outer appearance that he values. God's chesed is shown to people through the lovingkindness enacted by people. If this woman turns out to be generous, then God would have heard and answered Eliezar's prayers.

Chesed is a very important concept in the Jewish tradition. In Judaism, a person can be righteous, and still not be considered a "chassid" (someone who emanates chesed). *Chesed* is going above and beyond any requirement, any law, and doing so when you have nothing to gain by it.[4] It is an all-embracing lovingkindness that Eliezer asks from God.

When Rebecca arrives at the well, she appears as the embodiment of *chesed*, not only meeting Eliezar's hopes, but also exceeding them. We are told that she is indeed beautiful and a virgin, but those qualities aren't what impress Eliezar. He asks her for water for his camels. She, in turn, delivers the water to them and continues to do so until they are satiated—no easy task given the quantity of water taken in by camels! The number of verbs used in this very short space[5] introduce us to an action-oriented woman who moves at a dizzying pace: "She went down to the well, filled her pitcher, and came up." Soon after, we hear "and she hastened, and let down her pitcher upon her hand, and gave him drink. And when she had done giving him drink, she said, I will draw water for thy camels also, until they have done drinking. And she hastened, and emptied her pitcher into the trough, and ran again to the well to draw water, and drew for all his camels." What an introduction to Rebecca! She foresees the needs of others and, in goal-oriented rapid movement, performs acts of chesed by attempting to meet those needs. This is the Rebecca we will know throughout her life.

If we're lucky, then sometime in our own lives we will find friends like Rebecca. These are the friends who seem to understand what we need and, with a generous heart, go about helping us beyond what we would ever ask from them. Whether it's taking care of our dog when we have to leave town at the last minute, or making casseroles during times of illness or mourning or driving those extra carpools, their chesed is the spirit of Rebecca.

In response to Rebecca's generosity, Eliezar gives her lavish presents, including two bracelets of ten shekels weight. It's hard to bypass the use of numbers here. All numbers in Torah are considered to have deep meaning. Here, the numbers two and ten might represent the two tablets of the Ten Commandments.[6] Rebecca, a woman of *chesed*, may foreshadow the covenant at Sinai, by showing us the qualities God seeks in a people who enter into a covenant with God.

Eliezar then inquires if there is room for him at Rebecca's father's house. Again, she exceeds his expectations by generously offering not only a room but also straw and food for his camels. It is at Rebecca's house that we meet one of the trickiest men of Torah, her brother Laban. He is the greedy conniver who will later deceive Rebecca's son. Although Rebecca's father has no role in this story, in midrash he is portrayed as evil.[7] How stunning that in an idol-worshipping land, in a family that also produces a greedy conniver, a young woman grows up who will understand so much of what God wants from us! As in several other Torah stories, here we see a righteous person emerging from a spiritually and ethically arid home. Torah places responsibility on each one of us for human and spiritual connection. Our parents or our environment may challenge us or may even have hurt us, but in Torah we can find models of overcoming our limitations. Rebecca's story empowers us as adults to rise above the environment in which we live and not be destroyed or excused by it.

Years ago, I worked at a group home for abused and neglected children. Suzanne arrived at our home with a history of physical and emotional abuse, culminating in her expulsion from her home by her parents. Twenty years later, Suzanne and I had a conversation about her own parenting of four-year-old Eliza. She talked about the times when Eliza pushed all her buttons, and how she responded firmly and gently. I wondered aloud how she learned to mother so bril-

liantly given her own bleak childhood. Suzanne told me that when she was a child, she felt like a victim. But now, she had to make the choice whether to allow that trauma to take over her life, or whether to remember her childhood's yearning for a comforting, predictable parent and become that parent. She had to decide whether to keep being a victim of her parents' abuse by poorly parenting her own child, or to claim her life and become the adult she wanted to become. Suzanne felt that with support from a loving spouse and friends, she could move toward being that empathic parent. Righteous people can emerge from Haran.

The morning after Laban and his father agree to a marriage between Rebecca and Isaac, both Laban and Rebecca's mother try to interfere with her departure by proposing that Rebecca stay longer.[8] At this pivotal moment, I can't help but feel for Rebecca's mother. Not part of the original marriage decision, she has to let her daughter leave home, go far away to a place she does not know, to marry someone that neither mother nor daughter has ever met. How devastated her mother must feel, not knowing if she'll ever see her daughter again, not knowing if Rebecca's husband will be kind to her. How empty life could be without this outgoing, bubbling child! How will she deal with her life after this bright light is no longer around and she is surrounded by her deceitful son and unethical husband? Further, Rebecca is called a "naara," which refers to a young woman around twelve years old, or at the most, fourteen years old.[9] Her mother might feel felt that Rebecca is too young for such a risky venture. It is even possible that Rebecca is prepubescent at the time, and her mother might want her to wait until she reaches physical maturity before she enters married life. But Eliezar is on his master's mission and insists on leaving immediately. In response, Laban and his mother try another tack. They decide to let Rebecca choose whether to stay or go.

The tension is building. The young woman is called and asked by the people who raised her whether she wants to leave with "this man." It is a loaded question for a young teenager. Would she leave her mother who wants her to stay just a little longer? Would she leave everything she knows, everyone familiar to her, to go with a stranger to a strange land? Without skipping a beat, Rebecca responds "Aylach," I will go. In that one simple word, Rebecca shows us that she is just like her future father-in-law, willing to take the journey on faith. When God told Abraham to leave, he didn't skip a beat either. By taking this journey without doubt or pause, she defines her role as the spiritual heir of Abraham, the one capable of carrying on the covenant. She is the mover and shaker, the risk-taker, the doer, the pioneer. She will marry Isaac, the second-generation immigrant, the one who stays in the land of his birth, plants the roots, establishes a home.

Taking her nurse with her, Rebecca prepares to leave. Just like Abraham, she doesn't go it alone. Even when she chooses to take a life-altering path, she does so with someone she trusts and who could support her on the journey. At this point and perhaps for the only time in Torah, we are told that a mother blesses her daughter. Given Rebecca's certainty about leaving, perhaps her mother understands that it is best for her to go. Perhaps her mother realizes that it will never feel like the right time to say goodbye—when these days were over, she'd want her daughter to stay even longer. It is perhaps one of the most challenging tasks of parenthood—to know when to stop using our influence to alter our children's choices and instead to bless their choices. At some point, if her mother loves Rebecca, she has to take a deep breath and bless her and let her follow the path that she so wants to travel. Rebecca's journey has begun.

The next thing we hear is that Isaac came from Beerle-hairoi.[10] How amazing that he would come from that place to meet Rebecca! Beerlehairoi hearkens back to the days of Isaac's father's second wife, Hagar. Bereft, destitute, and feeling unheard and unseen by Isaac's parents, Hagar ran to the wilderness and was met there by a messenger of God. She was so uplifted by this meeting that she named a fountain "Beerlehai roi," meaning "for the God who sees me."[11] Isaac comes from this place, a place rich in the symbolism of healing and hope, to meet Rebecca.

Isaac meditates as he walks alone in the wilderness.[12] Then, as Rebecca approaches, Isaac lifts up his eyes and sees…camels! Not Rebecca, not a speck of the woman who will become his wife, not her maids or his father's servant Eliezar. No. Isaac sees camels. This reminds me of a memoir entitled *Misha's Story*.[13] When Misha was a child, she escaped the Holocaust by living in the woods, where she was cared for by wolves. When I heard her speak, she said that she sometimes still feels more comfortable with animals than with people. People caused her pain, while animals brought her comfort. Many traumatized people share Misha's feelings, and one can understand how hard it would be for Isaac to look up and be able to see people after his father bound him and raised a knife to him and after the sudden death of his mother.

But Rebecca can see. Not only can she see people, but she also seems to see the inside of people, to "get it" about people, to see others in all their complexity. So, when she looks up, she sees Isaac. She is ready and available for human connection. She gets off her camel and asks "What man is this?"[14] desiring to know whatever she can about her future husband. Eliezar answers concretely "my master," without any apparent insight. Yet, a closer reading can show us how much information the wise Eliezer gives Rebecca. He tells Rebecca that Isaac is "my master," not "our master." No hierarchy is set up between Isaac and Rebecca. This will be a relationship of equals, who together will find healing and laughter.

After "seeing" Isaac, Rebecca covers her face with a veil. One might think that Rebecca does this out of modesty. Yet, we have never seen anything modest about this young woman. After all, she is the young woman who greeted a strange man, scrambled to water his camels, invited him back to her home, and agreed to leave with him. So, why the metaphoric veil? Again, we see Rebecca as the relational visionary. She knows that Isaac is not capable at that moment of a totally revealing relationship, that he had been scarred by relationships, that care must be taken. She temporarily holds back part of herself in resonance with Isaac, in the interest of the relationship.

I think of my experiences with my friend's ten-month-old son. I would love to run over to him, hold him, tickle him, but if I approach too quickly, his lip quivers and I know that in a moment, he'll shriek and grab his mother. So, I sit at a distance and talk to his mom. After some time, he begins to crawl over to me—slowly and tentatively. If I move toward him too quickly, he'll scramble back to mom. But if I quiet myself, and wait for him to approach me, he'll eventually land on my lap, grab at my ear, and let me tickle him and hug him. Rebecca, in the interest of the developing relationship, is careful about what she initially reveals.

Isaac responds by bringing Rebecca into his mother's tent and making love to her, and she becomes his wife. We are also told that Isaac loved Rebecca.[15] This is one of the few times in Torah when were hear of emotional love between husband and wife. And, through this love, we are told that Isaac is comforted after his mother's death. His healing begins as he enters a relationship, but he could enter only because Rebecca understands that he needs her to slow down in order for them to connect. This isn't Rebecca's self-sacrifice, but rather a mutual relationship: Several times in Torah, we also hear about how Isaac demonstrates his love toward Rebecca. Mutuality means entering the experience of the other and being able to hold the needs of the relationship, as well as our own needs. For this relationship to develop and for Rebecca's needs to also be met, she has to move at a pace less familiar to her. And, our doer-and-shaker is capable of doing just that.

This movement in relationship reminds me of Steve and Connie. Steve, angry and hurt, told me that Connie refused his sexual advances. He wondered why she thought he was such a turn-off, and whether he could continue in a relationship when he felt so put down. He needed to understand that when Connie looked in his direction, she saw a camel. Her own past experience of sexual abuse made it hard for her to trust another human being and made relationships feel particularly risky. As much as she wanted the relationship, she shied away from it.[16] She was attracted to the witty, outgoing, loving Steve, but was scared by the vividness of his presence. Once Steve understood that this wasn't a reflection on him, but rather that Connie needed him to envision her predicament and be there with her in a way that she could tolerate, he could use his love and empathy to move at her pace. A gentle relationship slowly emerged that not only helped Connie on her healing journey, but also allowed Steve to feel a deeper connection than he had known before. Sometimes, all of us doers have to slow down and just be, we have to veil the enthusiasm and breathtaking pace of our lives, thus enabling ourselves to act in ways that are healing and connecting.

The relationship between Rebecca and Isaac is far from one-sided. Isaac is also able to show his love and commitment toward Rebecca. He is the only one of our original biblical forefathers who is monogamous. At one point in the story[17] Isaac almost repeats his father's questionable behavior by trying to pass his wife off as his sister and thus save himself from a jealous foreign ruler. However, Rebecca and Isaac can't quite pull it off. They laugh together and have such an intimate connection that Abimelech, the King of Gerar, recognizes the nature of their relationship and protects them. Most poignantly, Isaac is the only one of our original forefathers who prays on his wife's account because of her infertility.[18] His father Abraham didn't pray on behalf of Isaac's mother, and his son Jacob wouldn't pray in favor of Isaac's daughter-in-law Rachel, but Isaac begs God for children on Rebecca's behalf, and God responds.

Not only does Rebecca become pregnant, she becomes pregnant with twins! The joy she feels turns to agitation as she feels her twins struggling within her without understanding their unrelenting battle. I imagine this relational visionary assuming that people work through difficulties, and that they care for the relationship. So why doesn't her internal struggle stop? In a bold move, not repeated by any other female figure in Torah until Hannah, she takes her questions and concerns directly to God. And, in a response that again underlines the importance of Rebecca in Torah, God answers her directly. God does not chide her for asking so mundane a question, nor does God ignore her or send a messenger to speak with her. God speaks to her directly, telling her that two nations are in her womb, that one of them will be stronger than the other, and that the elder will serve the younger. Or perhaps that's not what God told her. Another way of reading the Hebrew[19] is "the elder, the younger shall serve." While God's words might be ambiguous, the meaning that we humans construct from God's words monumentally influences our lives. And so the twins are born, with Rebecca's assumption is that her second-born, Jacob, will be his brother Esau's leader.

We hear nothing of the childhoods of Jacob and Esau, and almost nothing about the parenting of these boys. We are informed that Esau is a hunter and man of the field, and that Jacob is a simple tent dweller. We are told that Isaac loves Esau because he values the venison that Esau brings to him, but that Rebecca loves Jacob. And here are sown the seeds of tragedy. As we will see, Isaac has good reason to love Esau, and Rebecca has good reason to love Jacob. But good reasons do not excuse overt parental favoritism. That favoritism will bring disaster to families, even families with the best, most sacred reasons for their favoritism.

Nicole, the young woman who tried to take on her sister's interests in order to have a relationship with her mother, had no contact with her sister Lara. Nicole reported mockingly that Lara was "perfect," while she viewed herself as irreparably flawed. Her jealousy and anger intermingled until she was no longer able to have contact with Lara. It took a great deal of work on her part, and a lot of courage, to recognize that it wasn't Lara's fault that she was favored any more than it was Nicole's fault that she wasn't. Later, she would learn that favoritism takes its toll on both siblings. Her favored sister felt she was always on the spot, that she always had to be perfect in order to maintain the image that her parents had of her, that there was no room in her life for experimentation because her position in the family was so clearly defined and too powerful for her to change.

Just as Nicole's parents had reasons for their behavior, so do Isaac and Rebecca. I imagine an only partially healed Isaac recognizing that his son Esau will never be the sacrifice; that Esau will always be the hunter rather than the hunted. What a joy for Isaac, what a relief! Isaac is drawn to Esau, the outgoing, powerful hunter who brings him food and nourishes him. I imagine the traumatized, broken Isaac who has begun to heal through the grace of his relationship with Rebecca. He becomes a father, and as Esau grows, Esau too takes care of Isaac. Esau prepares for him delicious venison, a concrete manifestation of his nurturance and love for Isaac. After having a father who almost killed him, what a blessing for Isaac to have a son who nurtures him! Isaac may finally be able to live up to his name, laughter, because of the love and nurturance that now surrounds him.

Isaac's favoritism toward Esau may also have other roots going back to Isaac's childhood. When Isaac was a young child, he had an older half-brother Ishmael, the son of a handmaid, who played with him and with whom he laughed. Isaac's mother, Sarah, feared that Isaac's inheritance would be shared with Ishmael. After hearing Sarah's concerns, Abraham sent Ishmael away and he became an archer living in the wilderness. It was years before the brothers would see each other again, and then they would come together only to bury their father. So, for his entire life, Isaac had to live with the unearned guilt that because of his very existence, Ishmael was turned out of the only home he knew.[20] Years later, Isaac fathers Esau who develops into a hunter just like his uncle, and who might remind Isaac of his wronged brother. How could Isaac not be blindly dedicated to Esau? Yet, while we can emotionally understand Isaac, we also know that being blinded to the reality that surrounds you can be disastrous.

And Rebecca loves Jacob, the man of the tents. She knows straight from the Source that the covenant will continue through Jacob. Since Jacob is a tent dweller, he is a youngster who likes staying near his mother. Rather than hunting, Jacob hangs out close to home, close to Rebecca. She therefore can spend time with him, teach him, and groom him to carry on his important role as covenant-bearer. Yet, even if Rebecca has good reason to support Jacob over Esau, favoritism still takes its toll.

So, when Esau is faint and starving, and his brother is cooking lentil stew, Esau asks Jacob for food. Jacob, possibly jealous of his brother's favored status with Isaac, refuses unless Esau exchanges his birthright for the soup. Since the birthright represents privilege and favoritism, it is possible that Esau with his nurturing and earthy personality does not value it. Further, Esau believes that he will die without the soup. He therefore agrees to the trade.

How deep the competition must be for Jacob to refuse to offer food—no strings attached—to his starving brother! Perhaps Jacob longs for a relationship with Isaac, and believes that if he has the birthright, that would force such a relationship. How sad it must be to crave a relationship with a parent so desperately that one would sacrifice a brother in an effort to scramble toward, to force, such a relationship. And how sad to think that one could magically have a relationship with a parent by stealing a birthright. Much to his credit, Esau leaves the scene not despising Jacob, but rather hating the birthright that drove a wedge into his family relationships.[21]

Rebecca knows that Jacob is the one chosen to carry on the covenant. She possibly also knows that Esau is not interested in that sacred task. Esau is interested in hunting and in nurturing. He is a devoted, generous and loyal son, and is even considered by some of our sages to be the best son that a father could possibly have,[22] but there is never an indication that he has any insight into faith, or any interest in developing a relationship with God. I imagine that Rebecca carries this knowledge as well. Therefore, this visionary mother not only considers it her responsibility to encourage Jacob to enter the covenant, she also needs to help Esau follow a different path more appropriate to his authentic being. This is not something that every parent can do.

I remember the arguments between Carl and Belinda about their older son, Harry. Carl expected Harry to join him in his highly successful family business. Harry, not unlike Esau, wanted to be a chef. No matter how much Belinda argued, she could not convince Carl that Harry was not temperamentally right for the business, that he had to let Harry go, that Harry had to pursue his own dream. It would take a long time and much anguish before Carl could begin to see Harry more realistically. Carrying on the covenant isn't for everybody.

Isaac might have begun to understand that Esau is not the person for the covenant by the time Esau chooses a wife. We are told that Esau picks Canaanite wives, which causes bitterness to the holy souls of Isaac and Rebecca who want their sons to avoid the "local" women.[23] When Isaac experiences this spiritual damage to his soul, he might begin to recognize the limitations of Esau's loving and uncomplicated personality. After all, the son who would become Israel must have the ability to struggle with critical issues, because Israel means "one who struggles with God and people and is able."[24] Is Esau capable of such struggle? Is he even interested in such struggle? Yet, because of Isaac's desire that this beloved son carry on his "family business," he might not have integrated that information.

Even after Jacob takes the birthright from Esau, there is still no indication that he has any relationship with his father. So, it comes as little surprise that when Isaac believes he is dying, he wants to bestow his blessing on Esau. We find out that Isaac is growing blind, although it is unclear to me whether his blindness is physical [25] or whether psychologically he is not seeing what could be plainly seen. At the same time, I would argue that Rebecca has vision enough for the two of them. Isaac can only dimly see that Esau is the wrong person for the covenant, while Rebecca knows from the struggle that she felt within her so many years ago that Jacob would carry this sacred obligation.

Rebecca overhears Isaac telling Esau to hunt and cook venison for him so that Isaac's soul will want to bless him before Isaac dies. Esau immediately leaves to honor his father's wishes. I believe that Rebecca knows that if Isaac were to die without blessing Jacob, without acknowledging Jacob as a worthwhile son, Jacob will be forever wounded. Rebecca will not allow this to happen. If Isaac is dying, the present moment could be Jacob's last opportunity to try to form a relationship with his father, and Rebecca will facilitate that connection as best as she can.

Perhaps Rebecca also understands that at important transitional moments such as this one, her husband once again re-experiences the trauma and vulnerability of his youth, and that being nurtured through food helps ground him in the present and thus sustain him. Food therefore may have a symbolic, as well as concrete, meaning for Isaac. Perhaps it hearkens back to a time long before, when a ram was sacrificed instead of Isaac, so that the cooked food represented to him his own reprieve. Perhaps it is because people often use food for nurturance, and eating when one feels most vulnerable is a response we can understand well. Either way, my reading of this story is that it becomes clear to Rebecca that if Jacob is to have any hope for a relationship with his father, it needs to be mediated by food. The question becomes what type of food could mark their relationship. What type of food can represent Jacob and therefore open up the possibility of authentic relationship between Jacob and his father?

Rebecca therefore calls Jacob to her. She tells him that Isaac just sent Esau out to hunt and prepare venison so that Isaac could bless him. She knows that Jacob is a man of the tents, not a hunter. For Jacob to present himself to his father as truly himself, as truly Jacob, he can't hunt venison. Instead, Rebecca tells him to bring two goats, an animal that better represented the man of the tents, so that she can prepare a delicious meal for Isaac. Perhaps she believes that once Isaac is nurtured by a food that represents the man of the tents, he could bless Jacob before he died.

Traditionally, it is assumed that Rebecca wants Jacob to pretend to be Esau, fool his father, and receive Esau's blessing. I believe it is just the opposite. Rebecca is there to help Jacob present himself to his father as the-most-Jacob he could be, bringing goat stew as would a man of the tents. Perhaps Jacob is to bring this food to Isaac because Rebecca understands that the food is what helps Isaac savor the present and escape from his traumatic past. If Jacob can bring the food that represents himself to Isaac who needs the food, perhaps they can form some connection and Jacob can receive some kind of blessing before Isaac dies. Rebecca never tells Jacob to take Esau's blessing, because that would not be the right blessing for Jacob since they are two very different young men. She does not want him to present himself with the same hunter spirit as Esau because Jacob has a tent spirit. She wants Jacob to be the-most-Jacob and connect with Isaac through the feeding and nurturing that enables his father to be the most-Isaac.

Rebecca is also not trying to trick Esau out of the covenantal blessing even though she knows that blessing must ultimately go to Jacob. God had previously given the covenantal blessing to Abraham and later to Isaac. It was not for Isaac to bestow. It is the human connection, the blessing of love and knowledge between parent and child, that Rebecca wants Isaac and Jacob to experience. But her plan does not work out in quite so straightforward a way. Jacob cannot imagine going to his father as Jacob anymore than Nicole could imagine going to her mother as Nicole. After all, throughout his life, his father has valued Esau and ignored Jacob. How can things change on his deathbed? Jacob wants to approach his father, he wants a blessing from the lips of his estranged parent, but Jacob can imagine approaching his father only if he pretends to be Esau, just as Nicole could relate to her mother only if she took over Lara's interests. But Jacob is worried. He has a smooth face while his brother has a hairy face. If he pretends to be Esau and is found out, he fears that his father will curse rather than bless him.

Another way of looking at Jacob's smooth face is by thinking of his face as naked. As we saw in the Eve and Adam tale,[26] one is most vulnerable when one is naked. We then cover ourselves up to protect ourselves against that nakedness, that vulnerability. Jacob can't face his father with the vulnerability of a rejected youth who desperately longs for his father's approval. He wants to cover himself up and appear like his possibly less vulnerable, more secure brother.

I imagine how crestfallen Rebecca must feel at that moment. She might be able to envision what Isaac needs and what Jacob needs at that moment. She might hope that the two would be reconciled before Isaac's death. But no matter how much insight she has, she can't get Jacob to simply approach his father as himself, as the vulnerable tent-dweller. She can't give Jacob the self-confidence to take that step. So, Rebecca answers "Your curse, my son, be upon me!"[27] She knows that if she proceeds to help Jacob get a blessing from his father, then Jacob's curse, his lack of self-confidence, will end up hurting her. Indeed, this entire plan will ultimately lead to her loss of her beloved Jacob.

If Jacob can't present himself to his father as Jacob, if he can only connect with his father through mimicking Esau's way of relating to Isaac, then she would have to help him because any relationship, she might be thinking, is better than nothing, and time is running out. So, she devises a plan. She dresses Jacob up in Esau's clothing, covers the hairless part of his skin with goatskin, and sends him to his father with the cooked goat and bread.

Certainly Rebecca couldn't have imagined that Isaac would be deceived with this plan. Isaac knows how his sons sound, feel, and smell. He is also a connoisseur of food and certainly must know the difference in taste between venison and goat. Further, goatskin is not going to feel like human skin. And, of course, Jacob is not going to sound like Esau. Our Torah tells us that what we hear is even more important than what we see,[28] so one premise in Torah might be that if we have a choice between believing our eyes or our ears, we should choose our ears. Jacob's voice will be an immediate give-away. The only deception here is Jacob's self-deception. Jacob, the trickster, is both the subject and the object of this ruse.

Rebecca knows that the only way Jacob can face his father is with the belief he will be "seen" as Esau. The only one fooled into thinking Jacob can pass as Esau is Jacob. And this gives him the strength to face his father. *I envision Nicole, desperately wanting a relationship with her mother and without the confidence to go after it on her terms. Instead, she joined her mother as Lara. But, her mother never truly felt that Nicole was with her, and she certainly knew Lara wasn't. They had to find a way of relating more authentically, but the first step was for Nicole to approach her mother in any way she could so that they could begin to bridge their estrangement.* Rebecca understands about Jacob, and helps him to move toward his father in the only way Jacob can tolerate:

by trying to deceive his father into believing he is Esau.

My heart goes out to this Jacob, and to all the other Jacobs today, who feel invisible throughout their childhoods and who learned to hide their authenticity out of fear and insecurity. I am reminded of eighteen-year-old Kayla who saw me for the first time during her freshman year at college. A high achiever, she was plagued with self-doubts. She thought she wanted to be a doctor--she had been drawn to medicine for as long as she remembered--but she feared that she wasn't smart enough or capable enough to succeed. When her parents asked her how school was going, she always answered that it was great, never revealing her troubled preoccupation. Kayla longed so to share her concerns with an adult, and yet she was so quick to put on the veneer of a successful, self-assured woman whenever her parents called. Kayla shared with me that this was her role in the family because her parents, due to their own tragic childhoods, found it unbearable to listen to her problems. They would minimize or just ignore the issues, and label her the girl for whom life was "smooth and easy." Adept at reading messages, Kayla realized early on that she couldn't be Kayla around her parents, that she was expected to be an imaginary all-happy, all-confident person if she wanted any relationship with them. And so it was, until freshman year when she could no longer maintain the façade and family therapy began in earnest.

Isaac, for all his errors, does not have the same issues as Kayla's parents. He gives Jacob several openings to admit to being Jacob, but Jacob is not confident enough to give up the ruse. After Isaac identifies Jacob's voice, he asks, "Art thou really my son Esau?"[29]and Jacob answers that he is. How bereft Isaac might be feeling at that moment—possibly recognizing that his un-favored son does not have the courage to face him honestly and directly because for all these years, Jacob has been non-existent in Isaac's eyes. Now, as Isaac's eyes dim, he has the first real opportunity to see what he has done and its impact on his son. So, perhaps he plays along for awhile. He asks for the venison and eats it, although of course venison and goat taste nothing like each other. He smells his son, and although Jacob is wearing Esau's clothing, he is also wearing goatskins and his body has its own unique smell, the smell of a man of the tent.

So, in that moment of both deception and sight, the moment when Jacob is least himself and when Isaac might be coming to see Jacob for the first time, Isaac chooses to give Jacob a blessing. Perhaps he feels some connection with the lost and yearning young man who stands before him; perhaps the dimming of his eyes allows him to reflect more internally.

Yet, it is only after Isaac feels the animal skins on Jacob's still childlike, hairless face that Isaac is able to bless him. What does Isaac discover when he smells the animal and feels the animal skins on Jacob's youthful arms? What might Isaac be imagining when he feels a young man who can be mistaken for an animal because of the skins? What message is Rebecca sending to him? Rebecca, with her acute relational vision, is possibly reminding Isaac of a time when he was mistaken for an animal, when he was about to be sacrificed by his own father. Perhaps she is reminding Isaac that there are many more ways to sacrifice a child other than by tying him to an altar. Might she be instructing him not to sacrifice this child?

The alternative to sacrificing a child is to bless him and Isaac begins with a blessing appropriate for a farmer. It has nothing to do with the covenant, nothing to do with carrying on God's word or the tradition of Abraham and Sarah. It is about receiving food and rain. And Isaac doesn't stop there. As much as he loves Esau, some part of him must have known that Esau is a nurturer, a hunter, a giver, but not a leader. Isaac continues the blessing by telling Jacob that he is the one who will be the master of nations and even over his brothers.

Moments after Jacob leaves, Esau returns with the savory venison. Isaac, the blind man who is now beginning to see, asks, "Who are you?" This is a profound question, and Esau answers it in his simple way by saying, "I am thy son, thy firstborn, Esau."[30] This answer, an answer that has honesty but lacks depth, an answer that acknowledges their relationship but gives no understanding of a place within the larger covenant, confirms what Isaac began to know earlier when his soul was embittered by Esau's choice of wife. When Isaac hears Esau's simple answer, he begins to shake violently. Isaac has finally begun to deal with the terrible knowledge that in spite of his deep love for Esau, in spite of the fact that his beloved son is standing right there in front of him awaiting a blessing, Jacob is the one destined to carry on the covenant. The blessing that Isaac already gave Jacob is minor compared to the blessing that Jacob will one day get from him and from God. Now that Esau is standing in front of him, Isaac might yearn to reassure his older son, but he can't. Isaac knows now what Rebecca knew all along, and he must say to Esau "and I blessed him [Jacob]; moreover, he shall be blessed!"[31] A heartbroken Isaac must tell Esau that not only did he already bless Jacob, but that the blessing isn't over yet, because Jacob will receive a further (and far more important) blessing.

But Esau is a simple man who loves his father and yearns for his father's approval. He is not seeking the covenantal blessing. He just wants a simple, personal blessing from his father and for himself. Begging his father for some recognition, Esau never once asks for Jacob's blessing to be withdrawn, but instead he sobs "Bless me, me also, O my father."[32] Although Isaac continues to say that he already blessed Jacob, Esau refuses to enter a competition with Jacob for Isaac's blessing. Instead, he continues to plead for just one blessing meant for him. It is as if a blessing is the acknowledgement that Isaac can see and recognize his son for who he is, and can articulate that vision back to Esau. Isaac concedes, and blesses Esau with a hunter's blessing. He predicts that Esau will serve his brother, but that when he tires of living under Jacob's influence, Esau would be able to "break his yoke from your neck."

For a period of time, Esau will serve his brother. He is furious with Jacob, and that intensity of anger can consume the person who feels it. Our anger can make us a servant to the person at whom we're enraged, and not allow us to spend our energy on any other task or relationship. It is only when Esau can let go of that desire to kill, of that rage that he can break his brother's yoke from his neck and go on with his life. Later, in Genesis 33:4, the brothers meet again and, weeping, they hug and kiss each other. The yoke would be broken.

But at that earlier moment, Esau was enraged and harbored murderous feelings toward the brother who seemed to have stolen more than a blessing--he stole a relationship that Esau had nurtured throughout the years. How often we see this scenario played out today. *Greta, a married woman with a high-powered job and teenage son, lived near her aging and needy mother. She drove her to doctor's appointments, made sure that she had the household assistance that she needed, took care of the day-to-day issues that arose, and visited frequently. Her younger brother, Bruce, lived an hour away. A doctor with two children, he visited his mother every few months, hosted birthday parties for her, and generously purchased a piece of new furniture to replace a broken end table in her living room. When Greta visited, her mother spoke about Bruce's generosity, her pride in his career, and his goodness as a son. Greta's contribution was never acknowledged. Greta, who had always sought her mother's approval, felt more and more rejected and exploited, and she found herself angrier and angrier with Bruce. Greta knew that Bruce never mentioned to his mother all the work that Greta did and never confronted his mother about her lack of acknowledgement of Greta. Not only did this destroy the relationship between Bruce and Greta, but it also consumed so much of Greta's emotional life that she felt herself to be a servant to her mother and brother.*

Esau has no plans to act on those hateful feelings during his father's lifetime, because his loyalty as a son outweighs all his feelings of vengeance. But he nurses the feelings and plans to get his revenge after his father's death. Again a visionary, Rebecca hears what Esau has spoken only in his heart, and she tells Jacob that he must go to Haran for a few days until his brother cools off. She knows that Esau is loving and simple, that he had never harbored a grudge, that he is hurt and furious but that in a short time, his rage will subside.

What a painful position for Esau! His mother can understand what he feels in the innermost recesses of his heart, and yet his mother loves and favors Jacob. How he must yearn for an expression of love from the woman who knows him so well. Yet, at that moment, both his parents seem preoccupied with Jacob. Just as Isaac might have felt that he lost both his parents after the binding, so Esau might be experiencing a parallel loss after the blessing. In both cases, an effort to follow what was understood as God's will without taking into account the feelings of the child results in deep injury.

Although Isaac has now blessed both his sons, he has not

mentioned the covenantal blessing. He knows that God will bless one of his sons with the covenantal blessing, just as he was blessed and his father was blessed, and he knows which son it will be. Isaac therefore is obligated to bless Jacob with the knowledge that he will one day be worthy of receiving that covenantal blessing from God. Isaac couldn't give Jacob that blessing while Jacob was trying to be Esau. The message would have been all wrong: you can't try to carry on the sacred message of God while you are not-you. Jacob has to be Jacob in order to carry on the covenant. If God wanted Esau, God would have chosen Esau. If God wants Jacob, then Jacob masquerading as Esau just won't do. So Isaac waits. He waits until the costumes are off, until the pretense is over, before addressing Jacob.

Following Rebecca's bidding, Isaac first tells Jacob to go back to Haran, to the land where Abraham and Rebecca were raised, to find a wife. With Jacob about to leave, time is running out and Isaac must share his understanding and wish that the covenant would be with Jacob:

"May El Shaddai bless thee, and make thee fruitful, and multiply thee, that thou mayst be a multitude of people; and give thee the blessing of Avraham, to thee, and to thy seed with thee; that thou mayst inherit the land in which thou art a sojourner and which God gave to Avraham."[33] With his whole family within earshot, with no deception, Isaac declares that Jacob is the one whom he hopes will receive the covenantal blessing. He also acknowledges in this blessing how much growth Jacob had yet to do because he calls Jacob a sojourner, a temporary dweller, in the land. The land represents God's promise and a way of living in the image of God, and Jacob will need to develop a great deal more before he can call that land his home. And that is what Isaac wants from his son: that he grow in self confidence and faith so that he can live as himself, in connection with God, a settled, full life. Isaac prays for the time to come when Jacob will develop enough confidence and faith to stop his sojourning and be worthy of inheriting the land. And, as important, Isaac frees Esau to become the man he is meant to be, not the one who has to stay in the family business just because he's the favored son, regardless of interest or talent.

At the moment he hears the blessing, Esau has to deal with the nightmare of losing his position of Isaac's favorite son. When children are raised to believe that one child is favored and the other is invisible, then the favored child is often vigilantly protective of his position. His fear is that if the other child gains favor, he will become the invisible one. But even as Esau is confronted with the new family situation, he does not give up on his relationship with his father. He uses that moment to learn how to be an even better son. He hears his father instructing Jacob not to take a wife from Canaan. Always the loyal son, Esau finally recognizes that his parents disapprove of his marriage to a Canaanite woman. Esau therefore decides to marry one of Ishmael's daughters. By doing so, he gives his father much more than any cooked venison. He gives his father a permanent reconnection with Ishmael's family. Through that marriage, Isaac is once again reunited with the brother whom Isaac felt was tossed away so many years ago because of Isaac's very existence. After years of separation, Isaac and Ishmael would share the same grandchildren.

So Rebecca's vision comes to be, although not in any way she could ever have predicted. Her husband is able to see her son and bless him for being authentically Jacob. Father and son can establish a relationship while Isaac is still alive. But the price will be a high one for her. Jacob has to go back to Rebecca's family in order to find the wife who can carry on the covenant, and Rebecca will not see her dear Jacob ever again. As painful as that must be, I

74

can also imagine Rebecca smiling as she watches her beloved son begin a journey that will help him find himself and his God and ultimately bring him home.

Notes

1. Rabbi Alan Ullman taught me the connection between Abraham and the entangled ram. An expanded discussion of the binding of Isaac can be found in Mirkin's article *Reinterpreting the Binding of Isaac:A Response to September 11*, Tikkun Magazine, Sept/Oct 2003, 61-64, and in Michael Lerner's book, *Jewish Renewal*, Harper Perennial, 1995.

2. Genesis 22:15-18

3. The Torah does not say that this servant's name is Eliezar. Our rabbis surmise that Eliezar was the chosen servant because he was Abraham's trusted and faithful senior servant, cf. Genesis Rabbah, 59:8; Yoma 28b, *The Babylonian Talmud*, Zohar 3:115a .

4. Maimonides discusses chesed as directed at someone who has no right to it. Chesed is "beneficence taken absolutely" (Maimonides, Mishneh Torah, Chapter 53).

5. Genesis 24:19

6. See Genesis Rabbah 60:6, and Herezeg, Y.I.Z., et al. (ed.) (1997). *The Saperstein Edition of the Torah: With Rashi's commentary*. Brooklyn, NY: Mesorah Publications, Ltd.

7. "Her father was a rogue and her brother was a rogue and the people of her town were, like-wise, rogues, and this righteous woman who came from among them might well be compared to 'a lily among thorns' (Song of Songs II:2)," from Genesis Rabbah 63:4. The Zohar III36:b, also considers Rebecca a righteous person who came from a wicked environment.

8. This is a foreshadowing of Laban's future trickery, when he deceitfully kept Rebecca's son working for him for fourteen years. See Genesis 28:18-29:30.

9. The word naara is used in Gen. 24:57. It is thought that Rebecca was fourteen when she married Isaac (Seder Olam Rabbah 1, Guggenheimer, H.W. (trans) (1998). *Seder Olam.* Northvale, New Jersey: Jason Aronson Inc.)

10. Genesis 24:62

11. See Chapter 2 for a more detailed description of this scene.

12. We are told that in this portion of the Torah, Isaac began the tradition of saying afternoon (mincha) prayers. See Zohar 1:132a, Berakhot 26b in *The Babylonian Talmud.*

13. Defonseca, Misha, *A Memoir of the Holocaust*, Mt. Ivy Publishers, 1997

14. Genesis 24:65

15. Genesis 24:67.

16. The Stone Center, and in particular Jean Baker Miller, Irene Stiver, Janet Surrey and Judith Jordan, call this a relational paradox. The paradox results from a desire to be in relationship combined with a fear of being rejected that leads us to develop strategies that disconnect us from relationship.

17. Genesis 26:6-11.

18. Genesis 25:21.

19. Robert Alter, in his 1996 translation and commentary on Genesis (WW Norton and Co.) cites Robert Elliot Friedman's suggestion that depending on the syntax, this line can also be read "the elder, the younger shall serve."

20. This interpretation is credited to Rabbi Alan Ullman.

21. According to Torah, Esau "rose up and went his way: thus Esau despised the birthright." (Genesis 25:32) Note that it does not say that he despised Jacob, a significant omission.

22. Rabban Shimon b. Gamliel said, "No man ever honored his fathers as I honored my fathers; but I found that Esau honored his father even more than I (Deuteronomy Rabbah, 1:15). Similarly, it is said that nobody in the world honored his father as Esau honored his (Zohar 146b), and that while Jacob was away, Esau spent the entire time honoring Isaac [Targum Yonasan, Bereishit, 32:12 in Maher, M. (trans) (1992). *Targum Pseudo-Jonathan: Genesis.* Collegeville, MN: The Liturgical Press]. Other rabbis have maligned Esau, although I don't find any evidence in the text of Torah that Esau was anything but loving and forgiving. For example, it is said that Esau means,

"Behold this waste that I created in My world" (Genesis Rabbah 63:8) and that he hated peace, Shocher Tov, 120:7 (In edition compiled by Braude, W.G. *Midrash on Psalms, vol. II.* New Haven, CT: Yale University Press, 1959). Throughout Shocher Tov, there are negative comments about Esau. In Shocher Tov 14:3, Rabbi Abba called Esau a degenerate.

23. Rabbi Alan Ullman (personal communication, 2000) teaches that the worlds "vatihiyen morat ruach" are used in Geneses 26:35 to describe both Isaac and Rebecca's response to Esau's choice of wives. He teaches that the word "ruach" is first seen in Genesis 1:2 and 2:7 to describe the "wind spirit of God" that prepares the world for creation and then makes our souls possible. That is why I called Rebecca and Isaac's "holy souls" bitter, because spiritual damage was done when Esau chose these particular wives.

24. Rabbi Alan Ullman, personal communication, 1998.

25. Many commentators discuss Isaac's physical blindness. For example, it is told that when Abraham bound Isaac, the angels wept and their tears dropped into Isaac's eyes, causing them to dim as he aged (Genesis Rabbah 65:10). Possibly connecting the physical and psychological, the Zohar (2:46b) tells us that someone who loves the wicked loses his eyesight. According to interpretation, Esau was wicked.

26. See Chapter 1.

27. Genesis 27:13.

28. "A voice of words you heard, a form you did not see, only voice" (Deut. 4:12).

29. See Genesis 27:24.

30. See Genesis 27:32.

31. See Genesis 27:33.

32. Genesis 27:34

33. See Genesis 28:3-4.

4

LEAH AND RACHEL: STRUGGLE AND COMPASSION

FLORA ENTERED MY office just hours after a phone conversation with her younger sister. Face taut, eyes blurred with frustrated tears, she reported the conversation. Flora had just received glowing feedback on her graduate school exams, her final step on a five-year journey toward her doctorate. The first person in her family to receive a doctorate after having been the first woman in her family to receive an undergraduate degree, Flora was particularly proud of the high honors she received. Excitedly, she ran home to call Eliana, her younger sister and closest confidante with whom she could unabashedly share her joy and pride. After all, the women were only 16 months apart and had been good friends as well as sisters throughout their lives. They had attended the same college, had a number of mutual friends, and supported each other through the many crises of adolescence and young adulthood. Flora was totally unprepared for her sister's response. "Why do you always have to brag about graduate school? Can't you talk about anything else?" Eliana angrily demanded.

Later, in my office, Flora fumed. Who did Eliana think she was? Here was Eliana, twenty-six and married with a beautiful baby daughter. Flora intimately knew every moment of the baby's daily schedule. She could tell you about her first smile, how her fingers curled, the way she puckered her lips before nursing. She knew the texture of Eliana's relationship with her husband—the lilt of their conversations, their favorite foods, the music they chose, the friends they met. How could Eliana tell Flora, an as yet single woman with no children, that all she spoke about was graduate school? Didn't she know what it felt like for a younger sister to talk about a baby when Flora didn't know if she would ever have one? When the family expected Flora to marry and have children before Eliana? Didn't Eliana know that Flora would have delayed graduate school indefinitely if she had the opportunity to be in a loving marriage and mother a child? What else was Flora supposed to talk about when school consumed her life?

After this outburst, Flora let go of the hurt enough to reflect on it. She recognized that she spoke to her sister not long after Eliana left a doctoral program that she no longer liked but was close to finishing. Eliana was always the more predictable one and the better student. She never left anything in her life, and while both sisters knew she made the right decision, and she was now free to choose a career course that would be fulfilling, there were the residual feelings about leaving without a doctorate, about failing a family that finally broke through the educational glass ceiling, about losing status. Flora, while still hurt, began to wonder how she could have been insensitive enough not to recognize what her words triggered in her sister. She wondered what stopped them from appreciating their own blessings enough to exult in the joys of the other. Wasn't their relationship worth it? Weren't they worth it? As she struggled, I saw in her story a reflection of the challenges faced by our foremothers, Leah and Rachel.

Every story in Genesis seems to teach us important lessons about what it means to be part of a family. In the Torah portion known as Vayetze, we are submerged in the relationship between the sisters Leah and Rachel, and come up with a luminous under-standing about struggle and devotion, about how the ability to stay in the struggle and see it through allows relationships to strengthen and flourish.

Leah, Rachel, and their mutual husband Jacob become the mothers and father of the Tribes of Israel. To this day, we are called the children of Israel, which can be translated as the children of the one who struggles with God and people and is able to stay in the struggle and see it through.[1] One could argue that in order to become the parents of the tribes, they couldn't leave relationships that become difficult, but instead learn to stay in the struggle and emerge wiser, more caring human beings.

So, struggling with oneself, God and people is not discouraged in Judaism, but rather is central to what it means to be Jewish. Struggle in Judaism takes on the meaning not of struggling against, but of struggling in service of the relationship. After all, didn't God often struggle with us and didn't the Divine One stay in the relationship with us through the struggles? As Rachel and Leah struggle with each other, they come to greater self-knowledge and a closer relationship with each other and with God.

The story of our founding mothers is radically different from the previous sibling and wife stories in Genesis. When problems occur between Cain and Abel, Cain kills his brother. When problems occur between Sarah and Hagar, Abraham sends Hagar away. When problems occur between Jacob and Esau, Jacob runs away and is not reconciled with his brother for twenty years. Each story takes a step forward from the one before it, but it isn't until Leah and Rachel that we learn an alternative to leaving a problematic relationship.

The fact that they were both seen fit to be our foremothers is also a change from earlier stories. Isaac and Jacob, but not their brothers, were given the responsibility of passing on the covenant. Sarah, and not Hagar, was permitted to mother a son who would pass on the covenant. Yet, in this story of sisters, both women are given the privilege and responsibility of mothering the Twelve Tribes who continue the relationship with the God of Israel.

Our story begins when Jacob approaches a well, that proverbial meeting place, in Haran. Jacob's mother, Rebecca, had urged him to go to Haran, the home of her relatives, to flee the wrath of his brother and to find a wife among her family and thus avoid marrying a Canaanite woman.

We know from earlier chapters that there are problems in Haran. It is an idolatrous, spiritually arid land, devoid of connection with the Hebrew God. Years earlier, upon God's command, Avram and Sarai left Haran, and Abraham would not let his son Isaac return there when it was time to choose a wife. Rebecca chose to leave Haran to marry Isaac, even when her mother and brother tried to convince her to stay. Haran was a place to leave, to steer clear of. How could Jacob hope to find a reasonable wife in that land?

However, our Torah demonstrates to us over and over that some people can grow and flourish even in spiritually stunted places.[2] Leah and Rachel are able to shine even in a place that is so spiritually and relationally bleak, perhaps because of the strength of their relationship. Leah and Rachel grew up together, and both became strong, loving women, worthy of being our foremothers. It is possible, even in Haran.

When Jacob first casts his eyes on Rachel, he is spellbound by the beauty of the young woman walking to the well with her sheep. Rachel is the only woman in the Torah to be called a shepherdess and is the biblical world's equivalent to the female engineer or the female construction worker. She is out in public, doing a traditional man's job. Sensual, free, beautiful, Rachel immediately captures Jacob's heart.

From the moment Jacob sees Rachel, he loves her. He takes her in his arms, kisses her, and cries with all the abandon of a lonely, scared young man whose life so far has held little meaning. This is the first kiss we hear about in Torah. This is the love Jacob had been waiting for, the love that would sweep him away from the loss and loneliness that came with running away from home and leaving everything that was familiar and everything that he loved. This is the love that would keep him connected to his earlier realization that God is in this place even if it appears to be spiritually arid. And Rachel, unfettered by gender roles, allows the kiss to happen.[3]

Jacob accompanies Rachel back to her home where we are first introduced to Rachel's older sister, Leah, and we are told, "Leah's eyes were weak; but Rachel was beautiful and well favored. And Jacob loved Rachel."[4] When I was a child and read this description, I felt sorry for Leah. I thought I was being told that she was plain, even ugly, and could never measure up to her younger sister Rachel. After all, Leah does not go out to the well. She is not a shepherdess. She is far from physically beautiful. I pitied this hidden-away sister. I saw her as the wallflower of the clan. But, my childhood understanding might have missed the essence of Leah. "Gdola," the word translated here as elder, can mean larger or greater. So, perhaps we are being told that there is something greater about Leah, some ways in which she outpaces her engaging little sister. Perhaps she is the one with greater spirituality, greater moral or ethical righteousness, or greater understanding.[5] We are told Leah has weak eyes, but another translation of "rakot" is sensitive. Kabbalist sources[6] imbue Leah with sensitive qualities, including understanding and inner hidden meaning.

We all know the quieter person who is very deep, who may not make us laugh as much as her vibrant, outgoing counterpart but whose qualities we love and admire. Our Torah is instructing us to focus on and value those qualities as well—not to pass them up just because they're less visible.

So, if Leah is a sensitive, spiritual woman and Rachel is active and beautiful, which sister should be chosen to carry on the covenant? After all, Isaac was chosen and Ishmael wasn't. Jacob was chosen, but not Esau. This story breaks with the past and makes a significant developmental leap. It is here that we recognize that there are many admirable qualities in both Rachel and Leah, and the Torah doesn't choose between them. Instead, Torah recognizes that we need this panorama of qualities to mother the Twelve Tribes of Israel. We need the actor/risk-taker/physical beauty and we need the reflector/spiritual being/sensitive one in our tradition. No person can have all these strengths, but between them, we have ethical, relational, emotional and physical leadership; between them, we have all the qualities we would want in the spiritual mothers of our nation. Whatever struggle exists in this chapter, the result is not that one sibling wins and the other loses. The result is not that one has power over the other. Instead, in a revolutionary new model, the sisters empower each other to become more of what they wanted to be, and to share privilege.

Jacob, smitten with love, asks Rachel's father Laban (who is Jacob's mother's brother) for her hand in marriage. Like Jacob, Uncle Laban is also a trickster. Unlike Jacob, he never grows from that position. Yet, his very presence is strangely reassuring, because this trickster has two remarkable daughters. Rachel and Leah aren't doomed because they have an unethical, unempathic parent—and neither are the countless other children in their situation. Laban tells Jacob that he can marry Rachel if he works for

Laban for seven years. Jacob agrees, but on the evening of his marriage, Laban clandestinely substitutes Leah for Rachel. Jacob wakes up the next morning to discover Leah in his bed. It appears as if Jacob spent the night making love to Leah and believing she was Rachel.

How is this possible? How could Jacob not know the difference between Rachel and Leah when he is in love with one and when the two are so very different from each other? Is it possible that the only way that Jacob could have been fooled is if Rachel participated in the deception? Could Rachel have possibly supported Leah in marrying her own beloved? I would answer yes, because our Torah seems to tell us that sisterly love outweighs all other love. Here is how our rabbis understood it [7] Rachel initially suspects that her father would trick them and wed Leah to Jacob, so she and Jacob develop signs by which he would recognize Rachel. Yet, when Rachel sees Leah disguised and on her way to marry Jacob, Rachel knows that in spite of all her plans, she could not shame or wound her sister by exposing her. Rachel, with enormous compassion and sisterly love, instead teaches Leah the secret signs. In that way, Leah could pose as Rachel and not be found out. The midrash pushes this point even further by saying that Rachel hides under Leah and Jacob's bed and speaks for Leah on her wedding night.[8]

Rachel's acts of loyalty and devotion are taken so seriously by our sages that they also tell this story[9] When the Hebrews were in exile in Babylonia, Abraham appeared before God and begged for their return to the land of Israel, but God refused. Isaac then approached God and pleaded for his descendents, and Isaac was refused. Jacob and Moses also took their turns to no avail. Then, Rachel spoke to God and reminded God of the time she let go of her own desire for the sake of her sister, and was moved by kindness rather than jealousy. Rachel continued, "So if I, a creature of flesh and blood...was not envious of my rival and did not expose her to shame and contempt, why should You...be jealous of idolatry, in which there is not reality, and exile my children...?" Upon hearing Rachel's words, God comforted her and reassured her that her children would return from exile.

Rachel's loyalty and compassion outweigh her immediate gratification and competitive feelings. The mothers of our nation demonstrate a value that will serve us well through the ages. *Not long ago, a high school student was seeing me in therapy and mentioned that a boy she really liked for a long time asked her to the prom. I waited, expecting to hear about her wish come true, but she spoke to me instead in the voice of Rachel. She told me that she couldn't go out with him because her best friend had been dating him for months, and that if she appeared at the prom with him, her friend would feel humiliated. She said that the friendship was more important than a date. It's rare that I hear someone make that choice. Maybe one day she will go out with this young man— Rachel did not lose Jacob forever—or maybe she won't. But what she did do was preserve her friendship and recognize that the friendship between women can support her for a lifetime and should be nourished and protected.*

When Jacob confronts Laban about the ruse, Laban agrees that Jacob can marry Rachel as well as Leah as long as Jacob works for him for another seven years, [10] perhaps a just consequence for all the trickery that Jacob had instigated in his younger life. Jacob weds the love of his life and commits himself to another seven years of work. While Jacob never says anything negative about Leah, the biblical narrator tells us that Jacob loves Rachel more than Leah.[11] Immediately following that sentence, we hear that God saw that Leah was hated. How can Jacob love Leah, albeit not as much as Rachel, and have God see this as hate? I would argue that we all know this feeling. To be loved secondarily is so humiliating and shaming that it can be experienced as more hateful than loving. We all know that to be loved less, to be loved non-mutually, feels like being hated. And sensitive Leah is confronted with this shame, this sense of being unloved, and this longing every single day as the outsider observing her beloved sister happily engaged with her beloved husband.

God responds to Leah's experience of feeling hated by opening her womb, thereby addressing the problem on several levels. First, women were valued for giving birth to sons, so this gives Leah an opportunity to be valued by Jacob. And, if Jacob doesn't value her even after she gives him sons, she would have the opportunity to feel loved by her children. Finally, we all know there is more than one way to love. One is a very physically passionate love, the intense, burning desire that is sexually driven and that Jacob experienced the moment he saw Rachel. Another type of love, often elusive, starts quietly and is built upon the foundation of a shared life, from living together, from raising children together. It is the type of love that Tevye wonders about in *Fiddler on the Roof* when he asks Golda, "Do you love me?" and she answers, "After 25 years of ...washing your clothes...if this isn't love, what is?"[12]

Leah seemingly understands this quiet love. I imagine it resonates with her more internal, deeply sensitive way of being, and that she hopes children will be a way of connecting with Jacob. Every time she gives birth to a child, she wonders if this will be the son who will awaken Jacob's love for her. She names her first Ruben, meaning "See, a son!" as if calling Jacob's attention to her and the family she is creating with him. Her second son, Shimon means "To be heard," because Leah acknowledges that God heard she was hated, and responded with this child. Levi, Leah's third son's name, is translated as "My husband will be joined to me," again hoping against hope for a connection with Jacob.

By the time Leah births her fourth son, she has learned a difficult lesson: Jacob still prefers Rachel, and all these sons have not brought her one iota closer to the man she so desperately wants. So, if she is going to survive emotionally and spiritually, she will have to find blessing in her life and not rely on Jacob to do that for her. With this, she names her fourth child "Judah," or "Praise God!." By naming her child "Judah," the spiritual Leah becomes the first person since creation to praise God. [13] This is the son after whom a kingdom will be named. This is the son from whom King David will emerge. This is the son whose descendents will survive when most of the kingdom is assimilated or destroyed. It is almost as if her understanding that this child is a blessing resonates throughout the centuries. Once she is able to see the blessing in the child, and not see the child as an instrument to bring on Jacob's blessing, she stops having children. Perhaps she can now begin to appreciate the blessing in each, and not simply accumulate more.

Just as Leah struggles with winning Jacob's affection, Rachel grapples with infertility, and neither is satisfied. Sometimes we see ourselves in comparison to others instead of appreciating all the goodness in our own lives. At this point in the story, Rachel and Leah each sees herself through the lens of what the other sister has and what she herself lacks. So, each feels lacking, and jealousy rages. Leah is jealous of Jacob's love for Rachel, and Rachel is jealous because Leah is able to have children and she is infertile.

I imagine Rachel, this spirited woman, this woman who is used to getting what she wants, waiting as her sister weds her beloved, and then waiting as Leah bears one son after another. Time is going by, she is no longer the young woman she once was, perhaps she no longer feels the youthful energy she once felt and perhaps she fears losing the sensuality that keeps her tied to Jacob. While Leah has children in order to support her relationship with Jacob, Rachel tries to use her relationship with Jacob to get the children she so wants. Rachel says to Jacob, "Give me children! If not, I will die!"[14]. Sadly, Jacob does not pray on his wife's behalf, as his father Isaac had done for a barren Rebecca. He does not try to comfort her as Elkanah will attempt to comfort an infertile Hannah (see Chapters 3 and 7). Instead, Jacob becomes angry with Rachel, implying that God is punishing her with childlessness.[15] Perhaps Jacob can't comprehend Rachel's longing for sons because he sees Leah as taking on the role of mother, of son-provider, while Rachel is his lover, the attractive woman whom he may not associate with being a bearer of children. Perhaps Jacob feels threatened at the thought that his sensual wife would prefer pregnancy and childbirth to a relationship solely focused on Jacob. There is no sympathy or support here. In a world that defines women as mothers or lovers, Rachel has her role. As a woman who wants more than a narrowly prescribed role, Rachel feels miserable.

Without Jacob to advocate for her, Rachel, like her grandmother-in-law Sarah, has to come up with a plan to obtain sons. She decides to give Jacob her handmaid Bilha as a wife, with the hope of having children through Bilha. Although she is not currently recognized as one of our foremothers, Bilha gives birth to two sons, two of the twelve tribes of Israel. However, unlike the earlier story of Sarah and Hagar (see Chapter 2), Bilha loses the maternity of these sons and Rachel names them.

Rachel names the first son "Dan," or "justice." What justice is Rachel naming? Is it justice that she obtains a son through Bilha? Is it justice that she now has an advantage over Leah? Perhaps Rachel feels too devalued because of her childlessness to recognize that this act tips the scales in her favor, leaving Leah as the unloved wife who is no longer the sole provider of sons. But perhaps Rachel's experience can't be reduced to a simple competition with Leah. After all, Leah has four sons and Rachel has one surrogate son and yet Rachel feels justice has been done. Perhaps what feels just to Rachel is that her possibilities are expanding: She can be mother and lover, she doesn't have to forfeit her right to children because she is the passionate wife, she doesn't have to be entrapped in one coveted role at the expense of another. Rachel also reveals that God heard her voice. This is the first time that Rachel speaks of a personal relationship with God. Perhaps, to Rachel, justice is that she can now connect with God in a way that seems to have always come more easily to her more internal, spiritual sister.

It is with the birth of Bilha's second child that I believe we reach a climactic moment in this story. Rachel names Bilha's second son "Naftali..with great wrestlings have I wrestled with my sister, and I am also able" (Genesis 30:8). In a great biblical moment two chapters later, an angel of God changes Jacob's name to Israel because "you have wrestled with God and with people and you [are able]."[16] Whether it is Rachel struggling with Leah, or later Jacob struggling with an angel/man, there is something about this struggle, and about staying in the struggle, that is holy and that allows for more connection with God and with people. Life is full of wrestlings, and when a relationship is worth it, we need to have the capacity to stay in the struggle in service of the relationship. Before anybody is qualified to be the parents of the Tribes of Israel, they must prove able to struggle and stay with it until resolution.

What does Rachel feel "also able" about? How does she feel capable of matching Leah's able-ness? It couldn't simply be about competing with Leah for sons because after Rachel has two sons through Bilha, Rachel never asks Bilha for another child even though Leah has four sons. Maybe she'll never have as many sons as Leah, but maybe that's not the point. Perhaps the outgoing, impulsive, sexual Rachel now sees that she is capable of staying in a relationship even when it is hard and that she can stay in a struggle and see it through. Perhaps she discovers in herself a patience that she never knew she had, a patience that is Leah's hallmark, a patience that enabled her to hang in there all those years until she discovered a solution to her infertility. Perhaps she feels seen and heard by God in a way that Leah discovered so many years ago with the births of Ruben and Shimon. Perhaps Rachel comes to peace for the moment not only with having fewer sons than Leah, but also with not birthing them herself. Although she and Leah have struggled, perhaps with Rachel's newly found knowledge, their relationship can now reach a deeper level, thus showing in everyday human relationships what Jacob demonstrates later in his struggle with the divine. This may ultimately not take away Rachel's longing for a child, but after this moment, she never asks Bilha to take part in a competition for sons.

As Rachel comes to this realization, Leah too displays empathy and sensitivity. After Naftali's birth, Leah notices that "she" had stopped bearing children, so Leah sends her maid, Zilpa, to have sons with Jacob. The "she" that stopped bearing children can mean Leah, or it can mean Bilha, since both stopped giving birth. My sense of Leah as a sensitive, insightful woman leads me to believe that she noticed that Bilha stopped having children. What might become obvious to her is that the balance is off between the maids Bilha and Zilpa. Bilha has two sons and her status is elevated while Zilpa has none. Therefore, Leah sends Zilpa to have sons with Jacob. She names the first of these children Gad, "fortune is come" and the second Asher "for the daughters will call me blessed." Since Bilha and Zilpa might be other daughters of Leah's father, Leah understands that by averting a competition between them, they will feel immense gratitude toward Leah. Once Bilha and Zilpa's status is balanced, Leah stops asking Zilpa to have sons with Jacob. She is not trying to win a competition, but to save a relationship between sisters. We can expect that if she has the opportunity to save her relationship with Rachel, she will take it.

We are now at a psychologically profound moment for the sisters Rachel and Leah. After Zilpa has children, we wonder what has changed between Leah and Rachel. On some level, nothing has changed. Leah still has sons. Rachel is still barren. Jacob still loves Rachel. But what might have changed them profoundly is their recognition that they can see a struggle through without leaving a relationship. Both acted from their need for justice: Rachel sent Bilha to Jacob believing it is just for her to have children, while Leah sent Zilpa to Jacob believing it is just to keep balance in the relationship between Zilpa and Bilha. Rachel and Leah both learned something about actively engaging in struggle for a relationship, and they are now ready to come together.

The opportunity is given to them when Ruven, Leah's eldest child, brings his mother mandrakes, which are herbs associated with fertility. The mandrakes were a sensitive gift from Ruven, who must have noticed that his mother had stopped giving birth. Rachel, who still yearns to have her own child, wants the mandrakes. This might create a problem for Leah: If she gives the mandrakes to Rachel and if they work, there will be an imbalance in their relationship with Jacob. Yet, if she withholds the mandrakes, she will unbalance her relationship with her sister and show a lack of compassion that has not been characteristic of them, even in their jealousy. Just as Rachel, according to Midrash, set aside her desire for Jacob years earlier to help her sister, so now Leah sets aside her desire for balance or even for more children in order to help Rachel. However, there is a difference this time. The experience of struggle might have helped each sister more clearly understand her own needs as well as empathize with the other.

The way that they resolve the mandrake issue culminates their struggle with an unambiguous recognition of mutuality, authenticity, and loyalty. Leah is clear about her dilemma. She tells Rachel that she feels Rachel already has her husband and now she wants fertility as well. What is left for Leah? Rachel immediately grasps Leah's dilemma. She doesn't defend herself or put her need above Leah's. Instead, she arranges a solution that would benefit both of them. She suggests that Leah sleep with Jacob that night in return for the mandrakes. Together, the sisters are empowered. Each gets something she wants and is also able to help the other. In fact, when Leah tells Jacob that he will be sleeping with her that night, she says that she "hired" him and Jacob does not even try to argue with the arrangement agreed upon by the sisters. This ability to put aside their competition and instead each authentically communicate her needs counters the trickery that comes so naturally to their husband and father and allows them to cooperate and shift into a win-win situation. Immediately afterwards, God allows Leah to have another child. Leah attributes God's beneficence to her decision to give Zilpa to Jacob, but God waits until the sisters resolve their quarrel before rewarding Leah with another child.

Flora had a choice to make. She could harbor her hurt and her jealousy of Eliana's marriage and child, at the expense of their friendship. She could ignore Eliana's comment, at the expense of their authenticity. Or she could let Eliana know the impact of her comment: She could share with Eliana how vulnerable she feels as a single woman from a traditional extended family; how unloved she feels as she watches Eliana holding her baby or cuddling with her husband. She could allow herself to take in Eliana's disappointments and shame about leaving her graduate program, and her fears about disappointing the extended family. And, she could allow herself to resonate with her sisters' feelings. And if they both choose the path of mutuality and empathy, they could possibly attain the resolution achieved by Leah and Rachel.

Soon after, Leah becomes pregnant, has another son, and shortly thereafter becomes pregnant again. Midrash[17] sees this seventh pregnancy and birth as yet another example of the compassion and loyalty between the sisters. At this point in our story, Leah has six sons, Zilpa has two and Bilha has two. Rachel has not given birth to any children. Leah knows that there will be twelve tribes of Israel, and she recognizes that ten have already been born.[18] Sensitive as always, Leah knows that if she has another son, Rachel will at most be granted one son. Leah resonates with her sister and empathically understands how important it is for Rachel to birth two sons. So, Leah asks God to allow her to give birth to a daughter (although I can see many other reasons to pray for a daughter after birthing six sons!) and to bless Rachel with a son. We are told that God remembers Rachel, and she gives birth to a son, Joseph.

Interestingly, this occurs when Leah is pregnant for the seventh time. Seven in Torah is the number that represents creation,[19] and whenever we see it, we know that something new and holy is about to happen. Just as Rachel gave up what she wanted most so that her sister could marry Jacob, so now Leah is ready to give up her greatest gift (having sons) to benefit Rachel. And, Leah does not share this prayer with Rachel. It is out of true compassion, an internal knowledge that it is fair and right for Rachel to be included as a mother of a tribe, that Leah goes about praying to God for her daughter. What is created here is a genuine mutual love and respect that will not succumb to envy.

Ever since she could remember, Cheryl knew she was golden at home. Her parents were proud of her high grades, they appreciated her interest in the multi-generational hobby of sailing that consumed most of their summer days, and they enjoyed the current events discussions they shared from the time she was in elementary school. Cheryl knew that her younger sister, Colby, felt isolated from the threesome. An adequate student, Colby did not receive Cheryl's top grades. Colby preferred the quick pace of water-skiing to the lazy glide and hard work of sailing. She was on the phone with friends through most of the current event discussions. Friends. That was the rub. Colby had so many friends, and boys seemed to flock around her. Cheryl didn't know how she did it, and felt unstylish and unpopular whenever she and Colby were together in public. She was so focused on her social discomfort that she didn't even pay attention to how critical her parents were becoming of Colby and how much they verbally compared the girls. It was only after she heard Colby crying on the phone about being the black sheep of the family that she felt a sense of remorse, a sense that she was participating in hurting her sister. Memories of the close times they had together years before grades and boys took on such import flooded back to her. She knew that if she were silent in the face of this injustice, she was supporting her parents' beliefs about Colby. That was when Cheryl went to her parents, shared with them the unfairness of comparing the two girls, highlighted times when Colby was blamed for something Cheryl did, pointed out Colby's strengths and how hurt she was, shared that she participated in scapegoating Colby because she felt so unpopular and wanted to be special in some part of her life. For that moment, compassion and sisterhood had won out over competition, envy and insecurity.

In response to Leah's generosity of heart, God not only supports Leah's desire for a daughter, but also opens Rachel's womb and she gives birth to Joseph. In Hebrew, the root of the word "womb" is the same as the root of the word "compassion." So, perhaps God opened Rachel's compassion as well as her capacity to bear children. While Rachel has the capability of showing enormous compassion to Leah, she also has her blind spots. When she thought it was fair for her to have children without recognizing the impact these children would have on the balance between her and Leah, she certainly was not compassionate. She might have been willful, outgoing and beautiful, but she needed an experience of taking into account her own needs along with the needs of another in order for her compassion to further develop. So, when she was able to acknowledge Leah's need for Jacob as well as her own for children, her compassion was opened and bore fruit.

Some time later, Rachel does have a second child, but this blessing is mixed with tragedy as Rachel dies in childbirth. She is buried on the way to Ephrat. Many years later Leah will be laid to rest next to Jacob in the Caves of Machpelah. Rachel, the wild, free-spirited shepherdess, is buried outdoors, on the road traveled by people. Leah, the hidden, internal, spiritual being, is buried in the cave.[20] Their burials are a fitting ending of the story and a final recognition of each sister's yearnings. Rachel, the one who spent so much of her life and vitality longing for children, is buried on the road where she can watch her children leave in exile and returned to their beloved Israel. Leah, who longed for Jacob even as she gave birth to each child, lies in eternal rest next to her beloved husband.

At peace with each other and with the possibilities and limitations of their lives, the sisters find their longings realized in their place of eternal rest. On the one hand, I am very moved by this fairy tale ending. On the other hand, though, it saddens me. Think of how much of Rachel's life she spent wishing for what Leah had and how much of Leah's life she longed for the love that Rachel took for granted. If only they could have enjoyed their blessings and celebrated the blessings of their sister, they would have experienced so much less pain on their journeys. In actuality, does it do Leah any good to be buried next to the man she yearned for but never felt loved by throughout her life? Does it do Rachel any good to be buried where she can "see" her children when she could not raise them into adulthood? How do we understand this beautiful and painful ending?

Perhaps we are being reminded of the journey. Leah and Rachel's journey was painful, but through hopes and dashed hopes and hopes again, they reached a place where they could be compassionate with each other and with themselves, where they could appreciate that which was given to them and reach out to give to the other. It took a journey of struggle for them to grow into women qualified to be the mothers of the Tribes of Israel. So, perhaps their burial ground doesn't need to be only a reminder of the tragedy of wasting years only to get what one wants too late. Instead, perhaps we can see two women—one laughing freely, hair flowing, beauty radiating, running into her husband's waiting arms. And the other. The other with the soft eyes, looking inward and looking toward the heavens, holding children and feeding children and hugging children. The women look toward each other with a look of knowing. They dream, but neither will get all that she dreams. But what they get is enough. In fact, what they get is more than enough, because they have each other and they have their own unique blessings. And through these two women, we too can feel pain, jealousy and longing, and we too can grow and end our own journeys in a more compassionate, knowing place than where we began.

Notes

1. Genesis 32:29: "Thy name shall be called no more Yaakov but Yisrael for thou has contended with God and with men, and hast prevailed." The words for prevail comes from the root of "to be able" which is offered as an alternative translation by Rabbi Alan Ullman.

2. For examples, see Exodus and the Book of Ruth. In Exodus, the daughter of Pharaoh is morally aware even though she lives in the narrow place of Egypt. Ruth is a Moabite, a tribe descended from an incestuous partnership and known for its immorality, yet Ruth is a woman of loving kindness and grace.

3. The biblical audience knew something of this sort would happen because the well, the biblical equivalent to a single's club, and water in Torah often represent spiritual, physical, or emotional birth. Eliezar and Rebecca meet by a well (see Chapter 3), as do Moses and Zipporah. Miriam's well is the Midrashic penultimate form of sustenance.

4. Genesis 29:16-18

5. Norman Cohen, in *Self, Struggle and Change,* Jewish Lights, 1995, says that "Leah was sensitive and kind-tender of spirit." (p. 129.) He writes that if the Torah was simply describing Leah as the older sister, the word "bekhirah" (first born) would have been used. Instead, "gedolah," the older one, also refers to Leah's greater spirituality.

6. These kabbalistic ideas are explored in Judith Antonelli's text *In the Image of God*, NJ: Jason Aronson, 1995

7. Megilla 13b, Baba Batra 123a, *The Babylonian Talmud.* Also, see Rashi, (Saperstein Edition).

8. Lamentations Rabbah, proem 24, *Midrash Rabbah.*

9. Lamentations Rabbah, proem 24, ibid.

10. Seven are the days of creation, so we need to be aware that something will be created at the end of any time period marked by that number. Here we have the creation of the family that will produce the Children of Israel.

11. Genesis 29:30.

12. Taken from lyrics written by Sheldon Harnick, music by Jerry Bock, 1965.

13. Genesis Rabbah, 71:5.

14. Genesis 30:1

15. Our rabbis tell us that God was angry with Jacob for responding angrily to someone in distress, Genesis Rabbah 71:7, Tanhum, Buber 7.19, Hasidah, Y.Y. (1994). *Encyclopedia of Biblical Personalities*. Brooklyn, NY: Shaar Press in association with Mashabim.

16. Translation by Rabbi Alan Ullman

17. Tanhuma, Buber 7.19. Rashi also recognizes Leah's desire to have a daughter so that Rachel can have a son. Genesis Rabbah 73:4 states that God remembered Rachel because Rachel knew that Leah was being given to Jacob in marriage instead of her, and she said nothing to stop the wedding. Rashi adds that God remembered that Rachel taught her secret signs to Leah. Perhaps when God heard Leah making a similarly compassionate plea for Rachel, God listened and enabled Rachel to bear children. We are also told that God opened Rachel's womb (30:22), lest anybody believe that the mandrakes could have worked without God's approval (see Zohar II:156b)

18. Unfortunately, women were not counted as the heads of the tribes, so the birth of Leah's daughter is not included in the tribal count.

19. Rabbi Alan Ullman shared this knowledge about the numerology.

20. According to the Zohar (II:158a), Leah represents what is veiled and undisclosed, so she is buried away from sight.

5

THE WOMEN OF EARLY EXODUS: BIRTHING AN ETHICAL COMMUNITY

IT WAS PAST midnight when I received a phone call from Jill,[1] then twelve years old. She was calling from a phone booth in a dilapidated, crime-ridden part of town. She knew me, although she rarely had a friendly word to say to me, because I supervised the residence where her brother and sister lived. Months earlier, an evaluation had determined that Jill would continue to live home, and now she, too, found herself on the streets after a fight with her mother. Both had been drunk at the time.

When I found Jill, her usual bravado was as shattered as the beer bottles whose shards lined the streets. Scared and vulnerable, Jill felt desperate enough to call me and to allow me into her world. We hung out on the broken steps of the community church for a long time, Jill talking, me quietly listening. As dawn approached, she agreed that, following the directions of the family's social work agency, I would drive Jill to the designated emergency shelter. When I walked in with her, a warm, friendly young man with a long ponytail greeted us and started to introduce Jill to the other staff members. I felt Jill tug at my arm and pull me aside. "I don't want to stay here. They're a bunch of hippies," she whispered frantically. I was surprised. I perceived the warmth of the young staff members and the caring atmosphere of the shelter, and I was taken aback by how differently Jill experienced the situation. The urgency in Jill's whisper was palpable, her fear just *under the surface. Legally, I could leave her at this shelter. She would be safe. But was there something going on beyond issues of physical safety? What about her soul? What about mine? As we will see in this story of early Exodus, to fulfill the teachings of our Torah, I was responsible for something more than her physical survival.*

In early Exodus, we meet Hebrew women and Egyptian women who not only defied Pharaoh at great personal risk, but went much further to insure the survival of the body and soul of Hebrew babies. What is the power in the story that makes it worthy of being remembered across centuries, and allows it to guide our lives today? How did this story teach me to leave the shelter with Jill, and join others in finding an alternative place for her to spend the night?

As we open to the beginning of Exodus, we know something remarkable is about to happen: A nation will struggle to be born. A nation that will be committed to a covenant with God and guided by God's commandments is about to emerge. Interestingly, the chapter begins with a struggle about another birth, the birth of Moses. It is not a coincidence that we meet Moses before he is born. His birth is a template for the greater story about the birth of a nation. We learn the ingredients for the birth of a nation by learning how this child survived in a hostile world. Survival in this story is not autonomous or independently achieved. Survival is possible when a group of people come together in a mutually supportive, empathic manner to develop a relational community.

Just as in Genesis we learned about how to develop family relationships, in Exodus we are given the task of developing a relational community. A relational community is mutually supportive and looks out for the welfare of even its weakest members. We learn the groundwork for developing this community from five women in the first two chapters of Exodus: Shifra, Puah, Yocheved, Miriam, and Pharaoh's daughter. It is not a coincidence that the protagonists of early Exodus are all women. Women give birth to babies and are socialized to nurture them into adulthood and teach them about care and commitment. They therefore are fitting models for Moses, who will help birth a nation that moves toward a commitment with God. These women are archetypes of righteousness and rebellion, of courage in relationship. In fact, our Talmud tells us that "On account of the righteous women of that generation was Israel redeemed from Egypt."[2]

Exodus begins with a genealogy. We are told the names of the twelve sons of Jacob (there is no mention of Jacob's daughter), and of the seventy souls comprising Jacob's family who originally entered Egypt. When I was younger, I skipped the genealogy. I found it boring. Recently though, as I found myself in the national archives tracing my grandparents and great-grandparents in the 1920 U.S. Census, I reflected more on the meaning of genealogy. I was once again impressed with the wisdom of our Torah in highlighting where we came from before tackling where we're going. The first step in forming our new nation is remembering our common history.

These first few lines give us another message as well. It wasn't simply seventy people who came to Egypt, it was seventy "nefesh" souls. We first hear about nefesh in Genesis 2:7 when God breathes into us and we become living souls, and then again in Genesis 12:5 when Avram sets out on God's mission (see Chapter 2). After years and years of slavery, how important it is to be reminded that the breath of God is in us, and that there is a possibility of life beyond servitude to Pharaoh. Remembering our connection with God, with what can be and not simply with what is, propels us forward as we attempt to form this new nation.

I have worked with immigrants who had been terrorized by their experiences in their countries of origin, and intimidated by the discrimination they faced in their adopted country. They taught me that a way of maintaining hope and dignity is to connect with the strengths of the culture from which they came, to hold on to their history and rituals, weaving together the old and the new into a bicultural experience. Every time one of the families with whom I worked celebrated the Cambodian New Year, they were remembering their twelve sons of Jacob and their seventy souls who entered Egypt. They gathered strength and hope through cultural memory, thus nurturing their own souls.

Curiously, in early Exodus we don't hear the voice of God and God's name is mentioned only once. This story is a template for human action, for human behavior. It is a story of what you and I and everyone else need to do to make this a better world. In doing so, we become models of living in God's image, acknowledging that the responsibility for behaving ethically in this world belongs to each of us.

With this introduction, we enter the story of early Exodus. We find out that Pharaoh has ordered the midwives to kill all newborn Hebrew boys. In the first recorded example of spiritual resistance to tyranny,[3] the midwives, Shifra and Puah secretly refuse to carry out Pharaoh's decree.

Who are these women? They are described as Hebrew midwives. Does that mean that they are Hebrews or that they are midwives for the Hebrews? We don't know.[4] My preference is to think of them as non-Hebrews, as the first example of righteous gentiles, an honored name given to non-Jews who risk their lives to save Jews. In our Torah, we often meet non-Hebrews who are wise and ethical, demonstrating that the battle for justice has no ethnic or religious bounds. The Torah may also be telling us that we are responsible for the human race, and not only for other Jews. If two non-Hebrew women can risk their lives by resisting Pharaoh, then what is our responsibility when we see pictures of starving children in rural United States, or children in lands devastated by floods, famine and war? What is our responsibility right here back home, when a child who is in distress is not our own child?

Torah tells us that Shifra and Puah not only disobeyed Pharaoh but also kept the baby boys alive. This sentence is ripe for interpretation. Why are we told both that they disobeyed Pharaoh and that they kept the baby boys alive when Torah is never redundant? Perhaps "disobeying Pharaoh" is a comment about their spiritual resistance—they disobeyed Pharaoh by listening to what God would have wanted from them. "Keeping the boys alive" might refer to their physical resistance by refusing to kill these children. Our midrash tells us that Shifra and Puah did more than simply disobey Pharaoh by not killing the babies. They also helped sustain the babies by feeding and clothing them.[5] The midrash is teaching us that refusing to participate in an immoral activity is necessary but not sufficient—we also have to take action to counter the impact of the immoral activity.

The obligation to care for the soul, and not just the physical being, of those who are hurt arises in our everyday lives when we aren't encountering personal risk. It guided me to listen to Jill's fear and leave the shelter together. We were able to make arrangements for Jill to spend the next day with me at a familiar residence. Shifra and Puah would have told me that it wasn't enough to leave Jill in a safe shelter, that I had to help care for her emotional as well as physical needs.

Of course, Shifra and Puah were found out. Pharaoh called to the midwives and asked them why they saved the babies. They answered that the Hebrew women are unlike the Egyptian women—they are so hardy that the babies were already delivered before the midwives could get there! Pharaoh believed this ludicrous story, thus teaching us a great deal about prejudice. When we are prejudiced against another, we reduce the other to something non-human. If we truly saw each other as human beings all created in God's image, it would be hard to be so destructive toward each other. Pharaoh had to dehumanize the Hebrews in order to abuse them. Because they were already reduced to animals in his mind, it wasn't strange to think they could give birth quickly and not follow the same rules as human mothers do in the birth process.

When I was seventeen, I spent a summer month learning French in a Swiss international school. There were only three Jews in this school. One day, a Norwegian friend, Kris, started playing with my hair. His look was so intent that I knew his action wasn't flirtatious—instead, it appeared that he was looking for something. When I asked, he blushed and told me that he was looking for my horns. He was raised in a community where there were no Jews. Jews had been reduced to something other than human, making it feasible to imagine us with horns. Yet, Kris knew me and liked me. So, he began to see me as more human and to question what he had learned. Furtively, he tried to check it out, and when he realized that of course I didn't have horns, he was embarrassed. The embarrassment, I believe, came from a self-conscious recognition that he was treating me as other than human, and that this behavior was wrong. Pharaoh certainly didn't have the self-reflective potential that Kris displayed. Pharaoh believed the midwives.

Once Pharaoh realized that the baby boys were surviving he ordered all Egyptians to throw Hebrew baby boys into the Nile. Every daughter was allowed to live. What irony! Pharaoh thought that by killing the males, he'd be safe from Hebrews. Instead, a community of relationally courageous women made it possible for Moses to survive and for the Hebrew Exodus to occur. The story continues as we meet Yocheved, Miriam, and Pharaoh's daughter who continue to demonstrate how we can support the birth and development of a sacred community.

Right after Pharaoh declared that the Egyptians must drown Hebrew baby boys, we meet a Hebrew couple. We are not told their names. We know only that they are of the house of Levi, the third son of our foreparents Jacob and Leah. Who is this Levi? We know that while Jacob ignored the rape of his daughter, Levi was one of the sons who avenged his sister's rape.[6] Therefore, we know that this couple comes from a line that is not silent in the wake of exploitation. We also know that Leah was a deeply spiritual woman. So, this family has roots in both confronting exploitation and experiencing spiritual conviction. But that is all we know at this point. The anonymity allows this Levite couple to be any of us. If we were immediately told that this is Moses' family, they would seem larger than life and out of our reach. But, Torah doesn't name them at first, perhaps allowing us to see that ordinary people can rise to the most extraordinary of occasions. They are us.

In Exodus 2:2, we find out that this woman, later referred to as Yocheved, gave birth to a son..."when she saw that he was a goodly child [Vateeray oto ki tov], she hid him..." The only other time we hear the words "ki tov" is during creation. When God noticed the divine creations actualizing their potential, God said, "it is good."[7] When earth brought forth grass and trees and fruit, God commented that "it is good," and when Yocheved gave birth to Moses, she saw that he, too, is good. Perhaps we are being shown that the birth of a child (and the metaphoric birth of a nation) is a creation as worthy of the "ki tov" as the beginning creations of

God. The awesome holiness of birth reminds us each time it happens of the miracle of God and creation, and of our co-participation in the continued creation of the world. My first response to seeing my newborn daughter was to cry—what else could I do confronted by the indescribable awe of that moment?

Yocheved, in recognizing her son as "good" through the use of the same words as in the creation verse, names herself as a co-participant in continued creation. As such, it is unthinkable to sit passively and await the murder of her son. So, she hides him until he is too big to hide. Then, she places him in a "tayva," an ark, much like Noah's in miniature. She places the ark at the brink of the Nile, and leaves. Her daughter, Miriam, stays to observe what will happen.

As Rabbi Ullman points out,[8] the ark is rectangular. It can't be steered by humans. Placing Moses in a rectangular ark in the Nile means that Yocheved has to have faith. She has to believe that God will steer this little boat. At the same time, faith is not the same as abandonment of human responsibility, so Miriam remains nearby. That intricate balance between being there and letting go, staying connected and allowing movement that doesn't include us, is played out in this scene by the Nile.

We all know that moment of letting our children go while still staying in connection. I remember dropping our younger daughter off at day care. She was two and began crying as soon as I said goodbye. I left her in the arms of a teacher. In order for me to leave, I had to have faith that she would be nurtured and supported for the next six hours. At the same time, especially at the beginning, I would drop by to peak in and be assured that the staff was relating to my daughter in a loving, responsible way. I was trying to find that balance between knowing that I couldn't steer the ark, and still waiting in the bulrushes.

But Yocheved's decision to place the ark in the Nile has meaning beyond its application to individual families. There are also lessons here about community. If Yocheved didn't know that there was a community of resistance to Pharaoh, could she have left her child there in an ark? Could she have taken a child whom she saw as good, and left him in a river overflowing with the blood of Hebrew baby boys? The leap of faith was more possible because Yocheved had already encountered Shifra and Puah, two members of this community of resisters. They demonstrated to us that part of forming a sacred community is joining together to raise a child by nonviolently resisting spiritual and physical tyranny.

In order for me to have left my child at day care, I needed to know there were teachers who would take care of her physically and emotionally. One of the most hurtful contemporary issues in our society is that welfare mothers are being told to go to work for substandard wages, and are asked to allow their babies to float in an ark down a river without the assurance that a loving child care environment is available to care for the bodies and souls of their little ones. As we will see in this story, it is a community, and not just a nuclear family, that is responsible for taking care of our children.

Let us now meet the woman from "the other side:" Pharaoh's daughter. In Exodus 2:5, we are told that Pharaoh's daughter went to bathe in the Nile, accompanied by her servants. Bathe in the Nile? The same river into which Hebrew baby boys were thrown and drowned? Why would anyone want to bathe in a river full of murdered babies? [9] Couldn't a princess bathe in the palace?

Perhaps this is a metaphoric washing. Going to the Nile River, looking at the perversity and horror, could be a conscious, deliberate act on the part of the princess. Perhaps she needed to see with her own eyes what her father was doing. However, Pharaoh's daughter didn't see only dead babies. There was a live baby crying in an ark in the river. Once she saw him, she couldn't turn around, go back to the palace, and resume her sheltered life. Once she saw him, she needed to wash the blood of this deed off of her own soul by taking action. Once she saw what her father was doing, she would hold herself complicit if she turned away and left the crying baby to die in the Nile.

Pharaoh's daughter asked her servants to fetch the ark, and when she saw the crying baby, she felt compassion and announced that this is a Hebrew baby. She didn't only refrain from killing the baby by noticing the Hebrew child and then walking away. Just like Shifra and Puah, she went a step further. She adopted the baby. Then the princess went even farther: She could be at tremendous risk if her father found out that she adopted a Hebrew boy. So, she could have pretended that this child was an unwanted Egyptian baby who was deserted by his parents and in need of a new family. She didn't have to put herself at risk of someone reporting to her father that she saved a Hebrew child. But, she chose to go public with an ethical stance. She committed herself publicly to not only to renounce the rule decreeing death to Hebrew boys, but also to take action to undermine it. Pharaoh's daughter, the child of the oppressor, teaches the nation that is about to be born that being silent in the face of injustice is being an accomplice to that injustice. Similarly our Talmud teaches us that saving one life is like saving the world. Indeed, saving this life was like saving our world. This child was destined to lead our people out of Egypt and into a covenant with God.

As the princess announced her discovery of the baby, a young Hebrew girl stepped out of her hiding place and approached the daughter of Pharaoh. Miriam, a simple slave, proceeded to ask the most powerful woman in Egypt whether she needed a Hebrew woman to nurse the baby. In a conspiracy of resistance, of refusal to yield to the immoral rule of Pharaoh, the princess agreed and Miriam introduced Yocheved as the baby's nurse. Pharaoh's daughter goes even further than simply allowing Yocheved to nurse her son. In a remarkable act of loving kindness, the princess chose to pay Yocheved to take care of her own child! Our Torah honors this noble Egyptian by giving her the privilege of naming the child. This baby, the product of a relational community and resistance to an ethic other than God's, is named Moses.

This Egyptian heroine is not named in Torah, but she is given the name "Batya" in our midrash. In this legend, God speaks to Pharaoh's daughter, saying, "You adopted a child that was not your own, calling him your son. In return, I shall call you My daughter." [10] Batya means "daughter of God," and indeed, she does demonstrate to us what it means to be a child of Eternal One. It means going that extra step, going beyond what would be considered the right thing to do and leaping to the most empathic, compassionate stance we can take. And, it often means working with others in our community to right the wrongs, to offer emotional and spiritual as well as physical sustenance. The woman honored with this name is not a Hebrew, and again our Torah teaches us that we all belong to a larger community of people, all made in the image of God.

Several years ago, I went to the Bat Mitzvah of my daughter's friend. She is a loving, smart, warm young woman whose mother died when she was a young child. Her father remarried a few years later and her dad and adoptive mom, Cynthia, raised her and her sister. Cynthia was not Jewish but went out of her way to raise this child as a Jew. Just like Batya, she made sure that this child was nurtured by the val-

ues of her biological mother. At the Bat Mitzvah, I was moved to tears by Cynthia's beautiful words. She said that her daughter would always have two moms who both love her and who both admire the young woman she is, that the presence of her first mom would be with her forever, and that both moms would be at her side whenever she needed them. Like Batya, Cynthia did not respond only to the physical needs of the child, but went a step further by keeping Yocheved present in her daughter's life. While so many people in our culture fight for the singular right to a child, this family shows us a sacred community. Batya and Yocheved could both raise Moses, and what a son they raised!

There is a strong cultural pull in the United States to "mind your own business," to give people "space," to "stay out." I believe our Torah tells us the opposite: That we are part of something larger than ourselves, and as members of a community, we have a responsibility to each other. When someone is in need, we are encouraged to offer our support and take that extra step. When my daughter was in fifth grade, I had planned to drive her and her friends home from school. On my way to meet them, I got a flat tire and it was clear that it would be a long time before I could get to the school. Sheepishly, I called the mother of two of the girls. This mother had recently had twins, and I can only imagine how exhausted she must have been feeling. She could have picked up her daughters and let the other two wait at school. She agreed to pick up the four girls. Then, she went even further and took care of all of them until I returned. This is a beautiful example of the mutual caring and responsibility that early Exodus portrays. This "going beyond" in order to take care of the larger needs of our children and our community is demonstrated in her exemplary actions. Hopefully, she also believes that the other parents will come through for her children. A friend of *mine[11] brought up the critical point that if that mother were tired or busy, it would have also been exemplary had she called another parent and asked him/ her to pick up and take care of the girls. The underlying issue is for us to be engaged members of a community where we have mutual responsibility for each other and our children. We do not have to feel that we are "superwomen" with responsibility to independently take care of everything that comes our way. Batya didn't act alone, and neither did Miriam or any of the other women of Exodus. They acted in a community of mutual caring and mutual responsibility. Together, they birthed a child who would eventually help birth a nation.*

The story of Exodus is the story of the birth of a nation, and starts with the midwives, in the service of God, resisting Pharaoh and assisting in the delivery of Moses. "Mitzrayim," which is translated into English as "Egypt," comes from a root meaning "narrow straits." The soon-to-be child crosses through narrow straits and is born.[12] Exodus grows to be a story of Moses, in the service of God, resisting Pharaoh and assisting in the deliverance of a nation. And always, the women of Exodus are there, saving, guiding, and supporting Moses throughout his lifetime, using their understanding of a relational community, their wisdom, courage, and moral certitude to help us move toward becoming a sacred nation. And every day, in our own lives, we are asked to continue that journey by accepting the mutual responsibility and feeling the mutual caring necessary to develop our own sacred communities.

Notes

1. This Chapter is dedicated to all the Jills I've been privileged to know through my years as a therapist.
2. Exodus Rabbah 1:12; Sotah 11b, in *The Babylonian Talmud*.
3. Michael Lerner used this term in *Tikkun* Magazine. See www.tikkun.org/magazine/index.cfm/action/tikkun/issue/tik0203/article020303a.html.
4. Their names are not Egyptian, but as Everett Fox tells us, the word "Hebrew" is usually used when foreigners talk about Israelites. See Fox, Everett, *Five Books of Moses*, Schoken Press.
5. It is said (Exodus Rabbah 1:15) that Shifra and Puah kept the children alive by collecting food from rich women to give to the poor Hebrew children.
6. See Genesis 34:25. Levi killed all the men of the rapist's tribe, a response that was so out of proportion to the crime that Jacob referred to this terrible act in his final words to Levi.
7. I was taught this interpretation by Rabbi Alan Ullman. He also suggests that Pharaoh's daughter made the conscious decision to go to the Nile, and once she saw with her own eyes, she could not simply turn away and return to the palace.
8. Personal Communication, 1998.
9. Elizabeth Mark, resident scholar at the Brandeis Women's Studies Research Center, argues that Torah never explicitly says that the Egyptians followed Pharaoh's command to kill the baby boys and that we therefore can't assume that they obeyed Pharoah.
10. Exodus Rabbah, 1:2, 1:30.
11. Harriet Lerner, personal communication, 1999.
12. See Chapter 2 for a fuller discussion of Mitzrayim as a narrow place. I would like to thank Gail Reimer, personal communication, 1997, for the parallels between the birth process and the Exodus.

6

AND MIRIAM DANCED: FINDING JOY AND SUSTENANCE DURING DIFFICULT TIMES

GABY WAS RADIANT as she stood on the bima, her spiritual presence breathtaking as she chanted Torah and sang prayers with a grace and delight that drew me even closer to her than I had already been. Gaby celebrated her Bat Mitzvah four years and ten months after her mother died and just as she was coming through two of the most difficult years of her life. All of us witnessing Gaby's Bat Mitzvah knew the tragedies that had confronted her, but few were prepared to hear her strong, jubilant words. What was it about Gaby that enabled her to sing and to dance with adversity so close on her heels? How did she express such sincere gratitude to God when times had been so hard for this young teenager? And yet, here she was, capable of being grateful for the moment, finding joy amidst hardship, and sustaining those around her. To know Gaby is to know her mother and sister, and to know her mother and sister we need to go back to our fore-mother, Miriam.[1]

We meet Miriam as the courageous, outspoken slave girl in Chapter 5 who was willing to suggest to the Princess of Egypt that she get a Hebrew midwife to nurse baby Moses. This spirit is the essence of Miriam's name: Rebellious Waters. Throughout her life, she represents water to the people of Israel: life-supporting, nourishing, and sustaining. Yet, she is far from a passive nurturer. Miriam is a rebel, willing to confront injustice, willing to find the joy that is not-so-hidden in adversity.

Recently, Jewish women have reclaimed Miriam. We add her name to Moses' as we sing prayers in our synagogues, we place her cup on our Seder table, we read books named after her well.[2] Yet, in spite of all the press that Miriam so richly deserves, she is rarely mentioned in Torah. We hear of her on only four occasions, and three of them are very brief. But in those short moments, Miriam captures our imaginations, pulling us to honor her spirit, emotional readiness, and ability to care for all of us, then and now.

Miriam is introduced to us first as a sister, and later by name and as a prophetess. She is never referred to as a wife or a mother, a stunning departure from the accounts of many other biblical women whose stories are so connected with their efforts to birth sons. But Miriam has no children and she has no husband, although she did take on the role of co-mother from the time her baby brother Moses was born. In midrash,[3] we are told that when Pharaoh pronounces that all Hebrew baby boys are to be killed, Miriam's parents divorce in order to avoid the temptation to have more children. Indignant, the little girl confronts her parents and tells them that they are worse than Pharaoh. The Egyptian ruler had ordered that the boys die, and Miriam argues that her parents are willing to deny life to girls as well as boys by their choice to divorce. At a tender age, Miriam already earns her name "rebellious waters" and her parents choose to remarry and birth Moses.

When Moses' mother places him in the papyrus ark and hides him in the reeds of the Nile River, it is Miriam who stays close by to watch and intervene in her baby brother's destiny. As Pharaoh's daughter finds Moses, pronounces him a Hebrew baby and chooses to save him, Miriam emerges and suggests to the most powerful woman of the time that perhaps she needs a Hebrew nurse for this little boy. The princess agrees, and Miriam brings Moses' mother to nurse her baby son. It is through this spiritual as well as physical nursing that a Hebrew identity, however hidden, is imbued within Moses, an identity that will take him forty years to discover and will lead him to be the greatest prophet ever to emerge from the Hebrews.

So, even at a young age, we find qualities in Miriam that will later lead her to her greatest successes and challenges. She is a rebel in the footsteps of God, fearlessly promoting life. She is dedicated to her brother and identifies herself as his protector, a role that will ultimately trap her and give Moses the opportunity to demonstrate the family love toward others that had previously been shown to him.

But now we're ahead of our story. At this point, we know Miriam to be the courageous and committed as yet unnamed sister. Miriam will be named, but first Moses has to grow up, move to Mideon and marry the daughter of a Mideonite priest, feel lost and desolate, search for meaning, and finally pause long enough to observe and listen to a bush that is burning but is not consumed. In his brilliant, life-altering encounter with the bush, Moses meets his God, discovers his identity, fearfully and reluctantly agrees to confront Pharaoh, and finally leads his people out of slavery.

Imagine the experience of the Hebrews. After 400 years of slavery, Moses comes to them with the message that God will free them from bondage so that they can serve God forever. Some are disbelieving, others afraid of paying a terrible price when Pharaoh's wrath is incurred. Plague after plague demonstrate to this frightened and dubious people that God is indeed powerful, indeed committed to releasing them from slavery. But just as the sand shifts in the wilderness, so shift the hearts and minds of the Hebrew people. And who can blame them? They are leaving slavery, but now feel like slaves to the wilderness. They fear starving to death, they fear capture, and they fear the heat and the thirst. And even though God protects them with a pillar of fire by night and a cloud by day, they are capable of feeling protected only for moments, and then the fear and uncertainty once again overwhelm them.

So they leave Egypt, which in Hebrew is Mitzrayim, from the root meaning "narrow" and they camp with the Sea of Reeds in front of them, and surrounded by places named Pi-hahirot, meaning "mouth of freedom" and "Baal-zefon," meaning "the false gods of the north." Surrounded by the freedom to serve the true God and the lure of false gods, the Hebrews have to make a decision that will forever change their lives. And as if that weren't complicated enough, they look back and see "Mitzrayim," the narrow place, following them! If that narrowness catches up with them, they are lost. If the narrowness catches up with them, they may decide that it is easier to go back to the familiar, even if that familiar is limiting and painful. But, if they do that, they will never experience the freedom of God, the joy and adventure of a life that they are just beginning to experience for the first time. Tempted by Mitzrayim, tempted by the mouth of freedom, tempted by false gods, tempted by the true God, the people remain frozen in front of the Sea of Reeds. If they could only cross, they could experience a rebirth. But first they have to enter the unknown knowing they could drown.

Moses tries to reassure them. He tries to tell them to be patient and God will help them. But the Eternal knows that the decision to cross into the unknown and away from the harmful familiar needs to be made by human beings, not by God. So YHVH responds "Why dost thou cry to me? Speak to the children of Israel that they go forward."[4] Once the Israelites are willing to commit to entering the water, once they make the decision that the Mouth of Freedom is more enticing than the Narrow Place, then Moses in accordance with God's words can pick up his rod and split the sea. And the Children of Israel journey through this narrow canal to be born again on the other side of the Sea of Reeds.

And when they have crossed the sea, probably weary and frightened and awestruck that they survived, that the path stayed open, that the waters didn't pound down upon them and kill them, at that moment in time, they see what must be beyond words to describe. They see the Egyptians crossing the sea, using the same path as the Israelites. They hear a great pounding of waters, the screams of men, the frightened whinnying of horses, and then a great, profound silence.

The silence must have been deafening. How does one react? How does one deal with seeing such an enormous display of power? With so many people dying in front of our eyes? With our own survival? With the multitude of feelings when we see the Egyptians drowning and we know that they are both our enemies and men with wives and children, men who are also made in the image of God. My guess is that they stood there and stared, frozen in time and space.

Until Miriam took a timbrel in her hand and started dancing. In the moment of our greatest fear, in a moment of being confronted with power that is not in our control, in the moment of seeing life and death and knowing that we are part of both, she responds with celebration. And all the women follow her, dancing through their fear, choosing life over death, affirming the Eternal, choosing to feel the blessing of the moment.

Who is this woman who can feel the blessing of the moment, feel it more than the fear or feel it through the fear? Miriam is introduced for the first time by name, and defined as a prophet and Aaron's sister. How strange. A prophet who does no prophesizing?[5] A sister of Aaron and not Moses? By understanding this description of Miriam, we may be on our way to understanding the woman who celebrates even with trauma looming.

Miriam may not say prophetic words or issue prophetic warnings to the Children of Israel. Miriam's dance is her prophecy. A prophet in the Jewish tradition is a messenger who brings God's will to the people. Miriam's message was coded in her timbrel. "Dance, sing!" The music cries out, "Do what finds favor in God's eyes. When there is a choice of life and death, choose life. At awe-inspiring moments, celebrate the moment, be grateful for it, find the blessing in it and recognize God in our celebration!"

But why is Miriam the sister of Aaron, and not of Moses? Perhaps those few words, "Achot Aharon," Aaron's sister, define Miriam's relationship with Moses. Although Miriam is Moses' sister by birth, long ago she had taken on the identity of a mother. Miriam nurtures Moses, she protects him, she saves him, she guides him, but we don't have a clue as to whether she gets anything back from him. What is Moses' responsibility toward this big sister? Aaron might be her peer, her sibling, but Moses is Miriam's child. And the skew in the relationship will lead to trouble, and will later in our story need correction.

After Miriam picks up her timbrel, she sings a short piece of a song that mimics the beginning of Moses' longer song:[6] "*Sing to YHVH, for He has triumphed gloriously; the horse and his rider has He thrown into the sea.*" Some biblical scholars maintain that Miriam's longer, richer song is lost to us and this short piece is the only part that is saved.[7] I envision Miriam differently. The Miriam whom I imagine is interested in bringing people to the point of dancing and creating their own songs. She reminds us with her words that it is our responsibility to honor God, to create songs and dances so that we can rejoice in the moment.

Several biblical scholars[8] believe that Miriam sings her short song before Moses sings the longer one, even though Moses' poem precedes Miriam's in the Torah. There are clues in the text that Miriam initially calls everyone, and not just the women, to sing and dance. She uses the inclusive/masculine form of "them" and of "sing." Perhaps the women are already dancing and she's instructing the men to join in this special celebration of the Eternal. So, Miriam tells the men to sing to the Eternal, and Moses answers "I will sing." Biblical storytelling is not a linear process, and this passage shows us that even though Moses' song appears first, perhaps it is the prophetess Miriam who orders all the Children of Israel to sing to God. Moses, portrayed as a great leader and as Miriam's child, follows her suggestion with his own glorious song.

The brevity of her speech does not take away from its passion. Later, when Moses learns to pray for his family, his prayer is also very short and heartfelt. Perhaps he learns from his big sister that it is our spirit, and not numbers of words, that glorifies the Eternal One.[9]

The Children of Israel, finished with their song and their dance, now begin their journey. They stop in "Shur," which can mean "to go out in a direction" or "to envision" and remarkably, they can't find any water in the wilderness of Shur. If we can't find water when we set out in a direction, then perhaps we don't yet have a vision of what will sustain us physically or spiritually on the journey. But Miriam is a prophetess; she is a visionary. She must have a vision of sustenance. And so, our midrash[10] tells us, a well of water is associated with Miriam. On the sixth day of creation, says our midrash, God created Miriam's well. It sustained our foreparents, and appears again in the wilderness where it follows Miriam and supplies water for the people until Miriam dies. Then the well dries up. This visionary has the ability to nurture and sustain others, to provide the spiritual well from which they can draw their water.

Before Miriam again reenters the text, Moses has a crisis of faith. Like his big sister, the overly responsible Moses keeps nurturing the Children of Israel on his own. Finally, he is so overwhelmed by these complaining, whining, scared tribes that he cannot go on. Confused and miserable, a beleaguered Moses reaches his limit and cries to God: "Why hast thou afflicted thy servant and why have I not found favor in thy sight that thou cast the burden of all this people upon me? Have I conceived all these people? Have I begotten them that thou shouldst say to me, Carry them in thy bosom, as a nursing father carries the sucking child, to the land which thou has sworn to their fathers? I am not able to bear all this people alone, because it is too heavy for me. And if thou deal thus with me, kill me...."[11] He seems to understand that a leader is a nurturer, but like his sister, he doesn't seem to know the limits of nurturing. He appears to view mothering/fathering as total self-sacrifice, until one is literally sucked dry by the needy children. Despondent, Moses wishes for death.

God, however, does not seem to view a world in which one person must take on all leadership responsibility, ignoring his own limitations and his own needs. God therefore tells Moses to gather seventy elders who have displayed leadership abilities. God promises to take the breath of prophecy, the wind-spirit of God that resides with Moses, and place it upon the elders who will then be able to share Moses' burden so that he has some assistance.

Moses still doubts his ability to provide for the people, but he obeys God and gathers the elders who all receive the wind-spirit of the Eternal. Much to our surprise, two of the men who are not chosen also begin to prophesy. Moses, rather than feeling angry or betrayed by the unchosen prophets, responds, "would that all the Lord's people were prophets and that the Lord would put his spirit upon them!"[12]

During this entire time, we do not hear from Miriam. How might we understand Miriam's experience? Her baby brother, the one whose life she had saved and whom she watched and cared for well into adulthood, is despondent enough to beg for death. Miriam is a prophetess; she is a sister; she is defined as nothing else in Torah. How can she relay God's will now? How can she save her baby brother once again?

In discussions that I've had about this text, several people have said that Moses betrayed Miriam. After all, he had to choose seventy elders, and he did not choose her. How could he have left her out? How could he be so ungrateful and so dismissive of her leadership skills? I do not think that Moses ignored Miriam. He is instructed to gather elders so that they can receive the spirit of God and assist Moses. Miriam is already named a Prophetess, the wind-spirit of God is already upon her, and she is already a community leader. Had Moses included her in this not-yet-initiated group, her role would have been diminished.

So Miriam has to decide what to do next. Whatever role she takes on will have to help ease her little brother's burdens and promote the values that she feels are so important for this infant nation. One of these values is the sanctity of family and family relationships. The fact that we rarely hear anything about Moses' relationship with his wife Zipporah must have troubled her. Although Zipporah once saved Moses' life, we don't get an indication that she is particularly important to him. When Moses married her and lived in Midean, we are told that he was content to live with his father-in-law Jethro. We hear nothing of his desire to live with Zipporah. We hear that he leaves her somewhere in the wilderness and that she had to find her own way back to her home. Later, when Moses is reunited with Jethro and Zipporah in the wilderness, after not seeing them for a long time, he greets and hugs Jethro. Again, we hear nothing about Zipporah. I imagine that Miriam, who loves and honors family, must feel so pained to observe her brother ignoring his faithful wife, especially at a time when her companionship and support could be so helpful to the despondent Moses.

Zipporah's predicament might be a particular trigger for Miriam because it may reflect her own relationship with Moses. After all, we know all the things that Miriam does for Moses, but up until this point, we haven't seen Moses act in a giving, loving way toward Miriam. Although she is always ready to support Moses, he does not seek out her advice or try to share his burdens with her.

So, they journey to Chatzeirote, an enclosure or village[13] for a people who have not yet bonded into a village We have a protective sister dealing with a depressed, overwhelmed brother, a brother who has a relationship with God but has less success in mutual relationships with family members. How can Miriam deal with the feelings brewing up inside of her? How can she watch Moses in pain? How can she help the lonely Zipporah? How can she bear her own anxiety about her family's situation?

Jenny, now in her thirties, was the daughter of a depressed mother and disabled father who had a difficult time attending to their children because of their own serious problems. Jenny was eight when her brother was born, and she immediately felt drawn to be his caretaker. Taking care of Sam helped both of them: it gave Jenny a focus on something life-affirming and took her mind off of her parents' problems. She felt useful and responsible, which helped her to feel more self-confident, and she felt loved by Sam, which filled her emotional needs. The arrangement initially helped Sam as well: There was

someone, however imperfect, to go to when he needed atten-
tion, help or love. Jenny was there for his Little League games
and to take him to the library. Jenny made sure that Sam's
favorite foods were in the house and that the torn shirts were
sewn. By the time Sam was in high school, he wanted Jenny
"off his back." He would yell at her that she was his sister
and not his mother. Jenny felt lost and devalued. She didn't
know how to devote her life if it weren't for Sam. She didn't
know how to transform from a loving parent to a loving sister,
and she felt unrecognized by her family for all her efforts. Yet,
the same spirit, resilience and spunk that allowed her to be
such a vigilant caretaker could now help her as she renegoti-
ated their relationship. And, if she saw her brother as a com-
petent adult, perhaps he could be capable of offering her
some of the caretaking that she so freely offered to him, and
they could finally find some mutuality in their relationship.

At this moment in our biblical story, Miriam is about to enter a renegotiation of her relationship with Moses, and the results are profound for both of them and for all the children of Israel. The drama begins to unfold when we are told that in Aaron's presence, Miriam speaks against Moses because of the Kushite woman.[14] Given what we know about Zipporah, why would Miriam be concerned enough to discuss with Aaron the relationship between Moses and his wife?[15] Our tradition tells us that Miriam is upset that Moses has stopped having sexual relations with Zipporah in order to always be ready and available to do God's bidding. Miriam's concern can be understood within the Jewish value system: after all, Judaism does not have chaste religious leaders. Rabbis and cantors are able to, and even encouraged to, have partners. Our biblical foreparents all longed for children and felt blessed by God when able to have children. Abraham had a child in his old age as a result of a deeper connection with God. When Hannah connected with God, she had a child after years of infertility. We hear that Isaac and Rebecca made love even though Rebecca did not conceive, and God blessed Isaac and spoke directly with Rebecca. Why disconnect from sexual relations in order to be available to God? Why leave a wife alone, in the middle of the wilderness, far from her Mideanite community?

This isn't the first time that Moses sees a connection between chastity and God. As the Children of Israel enter the wilderness of Sinai, God instructs Moses: "Go to the people and sanctify them today and tomorrow and let them wash their clothes and be ready by the third day: For on the third day the Lord will come down in the sight of all the people upon Mount Sinai."[16] Moses instead tells the people "Be ready by the third day: come not near a woman." In spite of all the women who helped birth and save Moses, who made it possible for him to enter a relationship with God, somehow Moses believes that he can connect with the Eternal only by keeping his distance from intimacy with women. And, given Moses' history of emotionally ignoring Zipporah, his distancing from her is probably not simply a sexual but also an emotional abandonment. My guess is that this estrangement both saddened and infuriated his passionate older sister. It is very difficult for Miriam to watch her brother render his wife invisible.

What does God feel about Moses' behavior toward his wife? We have no idea. God makes no comment. Notably, God does not dispute Miriam's observation.

Miriam and Aaron then move on to a much more inflammatory topic. They—and this time it's masculine plural, which means that both Miriam and Aaron are speaking—question whether God speaks only with Moses and claim that God also speaks with both of them. Why are they now questioning Moses' relationship with God and pointing out their own leadership abilities? There are many possibilities. After all, Miriam is still a big sister. She is concerned with her brother's fatigue, loss of faith, and sadness. She knows that Moses is willing to share power and probably sees herself and Aaron as having a close enough connection with God to help during this time of personal crisis.

Alternatively, Miriam might be challenging God and feeling dispossessed. After all, her little brother seems to be God's favorite. He begs for less leadership responsibility but still gets all the audiences with God. She tries so hard to take care of everyone and God has yet to recognize her. Is this fair? And what about Aaron? He is in the position of communicating to the people what God wants Moses to communicate. Yet, he is not their primary leader, and he couldn't even keep the people, or himself, from building a Golden Calf when Moses was off with God receiving the Torah. The baby brother, with God's support, is outshining his siblings. Why should this be happening? Don't the older siblings have a relationship with God as well?

And at this moment, God, the angry parent, storms onto the scene. God speaks to each of the three siblings and commands them to gather at the Tent of Meeting. Then God angrily lectures Miriam and Aaron, telling them that the Eternal's relationship with Moses is unlike the relationship that God has or ever had with any other human being. God speaks to Moses mouth to mouth, directly—not in dreams and not in mysteries or puzzles. Moses is the favored one—not the baby, not the little child, but the one with the capacity to meet God directly, to see the fire and not be consumed, to be in the presence and not die.

God's anger gives us the message that Miriam overstepped her boundaries both as an older sister and as one who serves God.[17] She became too involved in Moses' life without his permission. She hasn't envisioned him as an adult who has to make his own life decisions. When she and Aaron speak together, they act as if they are parents speaking about their problematic child. We saw the same dynamic earlier when Miriam stood by the Sea of Reeds and was introduced as a prophet and as Aaron's sister. Her peer is Aaron, and her child is Moses. And Moses is not a child. It's time to begin envisioning Moses as an adult.

Further, Miriam has always been a woman of faith, a woman who could dance at the shores of the sea. Yet, this same woman cannot accept God's relationship with Moses from which she and Aaron are excluded in spite of their devotion to both God and Moses. It just isn't fair, and she speaks out against perceived injustice now just as she did when confronting her parents years earlier. After all, her name is Rebellious Waters.

There is a delicious irony in God's response to Miriam and Aaron. Speaking directly to them, God insists that the Eternal speaks directly only to Moses. Perhaps the Eternal is angrily responding to their challenge of God's judgment while at the same time reaffirming the Eternal's relationship with the older siblings.

Finally, God is often seen in a parental role and God could be fed up with all this infighting. The Eternal might choose not to hear or accept another divisive word from the leaders. We can all flash back to our own childhoods as we hear God angrily calling the three children to come to God, lecturing two of them, punishing one and leaving in a huff. At least that's how a human parent might respond. But if God is the ideal Parent, then God is trying to teach something to all three of the children.

When God leaves, Miriam is white, stricken with a disease called zara'at. We don't know what "zara'at" means. Some call it leprosy, but there's no reason to make that assumption.[18] Miriam does not cry out or complain. We don't know whether she is too frightened to utter a word, or whether or not she is experiencing pain. We don't even know if she realizes she is ill. What we know is that the disease is evident to Aaron and to Moses, and herein lies the transformation. For Miriam to move back from her parental role, Moses needs to indicate that within their relationship, he has matured and is capable of advocating for the woman who was always able to advocate for him. God creates a possibility for Moses to move into that role.[19]

For the first time, Aaron and Moses come through for the big sister who has always been there for them. Aaron is so frightened by Miriam's disease that he apologizes to Moses, calls him "my lord" (not baby brother!), and acknowledges wrongdoing. What a step for Aaron! Not long before, Aaron was complicit in the building of the golden calf. When Moses returned, enraged about the golden calf, Aaron made up excuses and lies to cover up his behavior. Now, however, there is no cover-up. Aaron acknowledges responsibility for his sins and Miriam's, and he cries to Moses to save Miriam from this terrible fate. And Moses, who as far as we know has never prayed for or given anything to his sister, changes roles and becomes her caretaker. No longer playing child to her parent, he says simply and poignantly, "Heal her now, O God, I pray thee."

We have all experienced that moment when our worlds are turned upside down and our roles change. No matter how successful Dina became, she was always an adolescent when she returned home to visit her parents. Forty years old, a well-known lawyer and respected academic, Dina found herself in the same circle of interactions year after year. Each time, she sought her parents' advice, resented it, appeared to reject it, often took the advice, and then sought it again. Her parents readily offered help to their daughter, assumed that they knew better than she did, were angry and hurt when she appeared not to take their advice, and then doubled their efforts to demonstrate that they knew best.

No matter how well Dina knew the cycle, she couldn't break away from it until that terrible day in August when her mother was diagnosed with advanced ovarian cancer. Suddenly old, her father felt helpless and frightened. Her mother was stunned, in shock, struggling to process what she couldn't take in. Decisions had to be made. There was nobody to make them. Unless Dina filled in the void. Without wavering, without pause, Dina spoke with the doctors and then gently and clearly shared her thoughts with her parents. They nodded, they shook their heads, they couldn't decide, they placed the decision and their full support into Dina's hands. With great sadness but with more ease than she would have anticipated, Dina navigated the medical system for her mother.

God immediately responds to Moses and heals Miriam.[20] I imagine God's pride when Moses, for so long God's servant and partner, now shows himself to be a devoted family member. God then shuts Miriam out of the camp for seven days, perhaps because there is more that she and the others still need to learn, perhaps recognizing that she needs that time alone after experiencing God's fury, or perhaps still angry that Miriam chose to challenge the Eternal.[21]

Miriam has to be alone in the wilderness for seven days. Seven is the number of creation. Something must be created in those seven days, but what? What can Miriam learn in that vast place where, if we listen, we can hear God? How does she feel being alone after all those years of being surrounded by people? What happens to her that week? We don't know. Not a word in Torah gives us any clue as to Miriam's experiences, her thoughts, or her feelings. The creation of those seven days comes from us, from our imaginations, our experiences. Nine months before she died, my beloved friend, Marion Weinberg, shared her vision of Miriam in the Wilderness:[22]

Miriam, what was it like for you, there in the wilderness? What were you thinking, feeling, there in the nothingness? What was your inner knowledge? My questions may not be the usual ones that come to mind in studying this parashah. I am not concerned about punishment. I don't believe in a vindictive, punishing God. I'm not concerned with why Miriam fell ill and not Aaron. Some things we cannot know or make sense of. Rather, central to this parashah and central to my life and I think all of our lives, one way or another, is healing. Now as I grapple with illness and plant myself firmly on my own healing journey, Miriam has been my guide, like the cloud and the fire in the wilderness. Miriam, share with me your inner wisdom. If only I could know more. There's so little I know about your experience in the wilderness. What did you do there? Was it a scary place? Were you frightened? Were you sick? Was the water bitter? What were you creating in the nothingness? Did you know that everyone was waiting for you?

Some of these questions came up two weeks ago when I took myself to the beach. There, sitting on a rock, I started thinking about life and death. I started thinking about my dear family and friends waiting for me. I thought about how lucky I am in so many ways, and what a trying time this is for me just as it must have been for Miriam. But then something happened. I stopped thinking. I stopped wondering what Miriam was thinking alone in the wilderness, the nothingness.

Seeing the grains of sand, the earth and sea in front of me, I felt the rhythm of the waves. I heard their song. I saluted the sun and felt the sand, the grains of sand, beneath my feet. And at that moment, I knew what Miriam did in the wilderness. She danced.

And so did I.

And while Miriam dances in the wilderness, her previously fragmented children wait in the enclosure, in Chatzeirote, for their beloved nurturer to return. While we often hear of their complaining and their dissatisfaction, now their silence is deafening. They gather together, perhaps they finally form a village, and they don't budge. Traditionally, if someone is expelled from the camp, the group would keep moving and the person would have to travel on a parallel path, removed from all company. But nobody moves. Just as Moses and Aaron were finally able to show their loyalty toward Miriam, so now are the Children of Israel.[23] And return she does. Miriam arrives back to a group of people who no longer passively accept her sustenance and give nothing in return. She returns to a group that advocated for her, waited for her, showed their love to her. Miriam has good reason to dance in the wilderness.

How often our lives reflect that of Miriam and the Children of Israel. We go about at our frenzied pace, often forgetting what's important, often spending days so busy that we barely have time to speak to our partners, children, and friends. And then somebody gets ill and everything stops. Frightened, horrified, wanting so badly to have the time with our beloved that just the day before we took for granted, we wait. And, if we're very lucky, our beloved will come back to us healed. And if we're even luckier, we will learn and grow from that terrifying experience and never take for granted the nurturance and sustenance that the relationship offers.

And maybe, just maybe, our beloved and we can sing and dance in gratitude for yet another chance to make our lives a blessing. Miriam and Moses, their relationship altered, continue through the wilderness. We don't hear anything more about Miriam until after "The children of Israel, the whole community entered the wilderness of Zin."[24] Torah doesn't repeat itself without meaning, so if we are told that the Children of Israel entered Zin and we are at the same time told that the whole community entered Zin, then some commentary is being made. Perhaps we are being told that finally, they are entering not as a group of individuals, but as an unfragmented community. In a beautiful tribute to Miriam's seven days outside the camp, we find out that the Israelites have truly stayed together as community, and have not returned to the fragmentation that existed before they waited for their beloved dancer. Together, the Israelites live in a part of the wilderness of Zin called Kadesh, or Holiness. And it is there, in Holiness, that Miriam dies. In Holiness, Miriam is buried. And there is no more water.

I believe that my friend Marion also died in holiness. According to this chapter of Torah, dying in holiness might involve leaving this life surrounded by a non-fragmented community after living a life of singing and dancing one's thanks to God. Marion had her adult Bat Mitzvah only a few days after she was released from the hospital. She was so ill and so weak. And yet, even while her body betrayed her, her spirit found blessing. As she and her B'nai Mitzvah class waited for this holy moment to begin, Marion started to dance. And all the women danced with her. The community, connected by our love for Marion, stayed with her as she was dying and we came together when she died. And, at her daughter's Bat Mitzvah just a few months later, we all gathered together under a large Tallit, a radiant Jessica in the center, and with strong voices and linked arms, sang the Torah blessing. And we all knew that Marion was singing with us, and that Jessica, with her magnificent insightfulness and relational vision, would continue the journey and travel it well.

According to the Talmud,[25] Miriam, so loved by God, is taken by a kiss of God and not by the angel of death. She is the only woman in Torah to die in this way, and shares this special relationship with God with only five others: Abraham, Isaac, Jacob, Moses and Aaron. With that kiss, God communicates a love for Miriam as uniquely special as the Divine love for Moses. With that kiss, Miriam departs this world, and the well that once sustained the people dries up. Miriam is no longer there to nurture and sustain them. And the bereaved Moses, in a desperate attempt to find sustenance, disobeys God and hits a rock in order to obtain water and slake their thirst.

When somebody we love dies, our typical reaction is to feel that our water has dried up. How can we go on without our beloved? How could we ever find that love, nurturance, and sustenance again? The world feels dry and lifeless at those moments. If we are to grieve, we need to sit with our pain and our loneliness. We need to allow ourselves to bear the profound emptiness of the loss, and we need to know that we can't take quick action to heal ourselves. This is a slow, difficult process, and if we allow ourselves to enter and journey in this process, we can find ourselves desolate, but also discover that the journey is full of its own rewards. Moses' error is attempting to circumvent that journey by trying to feel better right away. Moses' response is so human and so misguided. As Moses discovers, if we don't allow ourselves to mourn, we can't heal and grow, and part of ourselves ends up dying in that wilderness.

So we meet Miriam only four times, and yet she captures our imaginations like no other biblical woman. Many of us pay homage to her ability to sustain her faith by placing a cup of Miriam, a cup of life-sustaining water, on our Seder tables. We place her painted tambourines in our living rooms, and some of us sing songs about her and claim her in our "Mi Chamocha" prayers. In actuality, we know very little about this woman, but we do know that she could stand up to those in power, and unite with another woman in protest against misuse of power. We know that she could be in the moment, even as life throws us and scares us. She could dance and sing and thank God because there is so much good, so much to be thankful for, in our imperfect world. Miriam is our prophet, our messenger of God, calling us not to expect an easy life, but to rise and sing and dance on our journey through our own treacherous and blessed wilderness.

Notes

1. This chapter is dedicated with love to my friend Marion Weinberg, may her name be a blessing, and to her daughters Jessica and Gabrielle. Their true names are being used in this chapter.

2. Rabbi Susan Schnur, Matia Rania Angelou and Janet Burkenfeld suggest seder rituals that include Miriam's cup. See Schwartz, R. (ed) (2001). *All the Women Followed Her: A Collection of Writings on Miriam the Prophet and the Women of Exodus.* Mountain View, CA: Rikudai Miriam Press; see also Penina Adelman's book *Miriam's Well* and her article in *Moment* magazine (August 1997).

3. Sotah 12a.

4. Exodus 14:15

5. R. Herezeg, Y.I.Z., et. al. (ed.) (1997). *The Saperstein Edition of the Torah: With Rashi's Commentary.* Brooklyn, NY: Mesorah Publications, Ltd., argues that Miriam was a prophetess only before Moses was born, and then her prophecy was given to Moses. However, this is unlikely since she is introduced as a prophetess for the first time when Moses is already an adult.

6. Exodus 15:1-21

7. cf: Brenner and Van Dijk-Hemmes in *On Gendering Texts: Female and Male Voices in the Hebrew Bible"* E.J. Brill, NY: 1993, quoted Phyllis Trible as saying that the biblical redactors reassigned Miriam's song to Moses (Trible, 1989, p. 20).

8. cf: Janzen; also ibid, p. 40.

9. The spirit that Miriam imbues in all the Israelites is possibly why she captured the imagination of our prophet Mica. At a time when women were often ignored, Mica (6:4) said, "For I brought you up from the land of Egypt and redeemed you from the house of bondage and I set before you Moses, Aaron and Miriam."

10. Numbers Rabbah 1:2; Pirke de Rabbi Eliezer, *The Babylonian Talmud,*

Chapter 18.

11. Numbers, 11:11-15.

12. Numbers 11:29

13. Rabbi David Wilfond provided this translation of Chatzeirote.

14. The translation of this verse often indicates that both Miriam and Aaron spoke against Moses. However, the verb "vitaber" is feminine singular, and therefore it appears that Miriam is the one who spoke. Scholars have argued the meaning of Kushite woman. Some believe that she is a woman from Kush, or Ethiopia. (See Weems, R. 1988. *Just a Sister Away.* San Diego, CA: Lura Media). Some of these scholars believe that Miriam and Aaron were upset that Moses married a black woman. However, this is unlikely for a number of reasons. First, they are making the assumption that Moses and Miriam were white, and there is no reason for that assumption. Second, the word Kushite and the word beautiful have the same numerical value in Hebrew, indicating that the tradition sees Ethiopian women as beautiful and does not posit any racial inferiority. It is more likely that Kushite means from Kushan, which is another word for Midean (Habbukuk 3:7), and therefore suggests that Miriam and Aaron were upset because of Zipporah.

15. Renita Weems, ibid, makes the interesting argument that Miriam was envious and insecure because she feared that Moses would be less attentive and accessible to her due to his marriage. While I find her chapter fascinating, and I see her book as an important addition to feminist understanding of Bible, I do not think there is any biblical indication that Moses paid enough attention to Zipporah for her to be a threat to Miriam. Alternatively, Rashi tells of the two men who said they could prophesy. According to Rashi, when Zipporah hears of these men's change in status, she exclaims that she pities their wives because the husbands will separate from them just as Moses separated from her. Miriam overhears Zipporah's statement and recognizes that Zipporah is being treated poorly. According to Rashi, Miriam said that she and Aaron continue to have relations with their spouses in spite of receiving messages from God. Similarly in Beha'aloscha 738, *The Babylonian Talmud*, Zipporah tells Miriam that she feels sorry for the wives of the newly appointed elders because the elders will separate from them.

16. Exodus 19:10-11 and Exodus 19:15.

17. Many of the traditional interpretations assume that God is angry with Miriam for "lashon harah," for a bad tongue or for gossiping against Moses.

18. Rashi states that Miriam was covered with leprosy because that is God's punishment for slander. Deuteronomy Rabbah 6:8 defends Miriam and says that she wanted Moses to have relations with his wife and father more children. If she was punished so severely for this minor action, Deuteronomy Rabbah warns that people should beware of publicly speaking against another person.

19. Rashi suggests that God would forgive Miriam and Moses only if Moses first forgave them and if Moses wanted them to be forgiven by God.

20. Deuteronomy Rabbah 6:13 portrays Moses as a very strong advocate for Miriam: Moses tells God that the Eternal has made him a doctor, so that if God doesn't heal Miriam, Moses will!

21. While some argue that Miriam had leprosy for a week, this is unlikely because people who have skin diseases are not allowed back for seven days after they are healed. Therefore, for Miriam to rejoin the group after a week, she must have been instantly healed.

22. This dvar was delivered by Marion at her adult Bat Mitzvah in June, 1997 and was subsequently published in Schwartz, R. (2001). *All the Women Followed Her.* Rikudei Miriam Press, 2001.

23. Rashi tells us that God rewarded Miriam for waiting beside Moses when he was in the Nile by having the Children of Israel wait for Miriam when she was outside the camp for seven days.

24. I would like to thank Bonna Haberman for her translation of "kol-eida" as entire community. The quote is taken from Numbers 20:1.

25. Baba Batra, 17a, *The Babylonian Talmud.*

7

HANNAH: VOICE, FREEDOM AND GRACE

I THINK BACK to that humid August day eight years ago when Liz entered my office, her face paler, her too-thin body thinner than usual. Her large green eyes, partially obscured by the brown shadows encasing them, loomed even larger because of the emaciated cheekbones beneath them. She sat down quietly, and looked toward the floor. We sat in silence for a long time, as I tried to avert my own eyes from her twig-like fingers that were in perpetual motion, fingering the brown wool sweater that she wore on this summer's day. I knew to wait, and that Liz would summon her voice and speak her truths. It hadn't always been like that. For a long time, Liz was so disconnected from her inner knowledge that she would be silent, but slowly and painstakingly, she searched inside, and the silence was replaced by abrupt then flowing words, falling out, halting, moving. This time Liz told me that two days earlier she had been at the beach and from the distance, she had seen a friend and her new baby. Liz had been trying to have a baby for five years. As all her friends and her siblings entered graduate school and worked their way up the career ladder, Liz had gotten married and taken a job at a local preschool. She bided her time, waiting to have her own children and to leave the school to raise them. Five years passed and Liz found herself approaching thirty and childless. On that summer day, her pain was unbearable as she saw her friend begin to nurse the baby, and she fled from the beach. She didn't say anything to her husband or friends because "What's there to say?" She avoided speaking to an aunt who called because she feared hearing the question, "So when are we going to hear some good news already?" She refused to eat anything more than a few cups of lettuce for the next two days.

Eight years later, I remember this conversation as I reread the Christmas card that I had just received from Liz. I look at the pictures of the two laughing little boys, ages 6 and 4, and the baby girl, adopted just a month earlier. I know I will hear in beautiful detail about each of these three little ones. I know I will also read about the educational groups that Liz runs for teachers and parents about adoptive children, and I know I will feel a surge of emotion as I resonate with the passion she feels about her children, her partner and her work. And I know that whenever I get a card from Liz, I will think of her soul mate, the biblical Hannah.

As we enter the Book of Samuel, it seems as though we are about to meet the ideal (albeit polygamist) family. First, we are introduced to a man named Elkana. Since his name means "God acquired," we immediately wonder what God will acquire in this story and what meaning that will have. We are also told that Elkana has wives named Hannah, meaning grace, and Penina, meaning pearl, and that they live in a place called "Two Heights Look-Out." Since "look-out" is thought by some to be a Hebrew term for prophets,[1] we know that this family is living in a breeding ground for prophets. So far, life seems idyllic for this little family. A man whose name reflects some relationship with God, Elkana lives in a holy place with one wife full of grace and another full of beauty and hidden value. What could mar this perfect fairy tale beginning? Torah doesn't take long to tell us.

In the next part of the sentence, we hear that Penina has children, and Hannah has no children. A pall immediately falls over us, as it does over their household. So many women can tell us what it is like to want children, to try to become pregnant month after month, year after year, or to try to adopt and find that the lists are so long that you just don't believe the baby will ever arrive. But to then share your house with a mother who has many young children? How many of us have difficulty even being friends with someone who has children while we are dealing with infertility, never mind sharing every meal with another mother and her babies?

And this isn't only about children. Whenever we want something with all our heart and soul so that it becomes the singular purpose of our lives, it is so painfully difficult to share a physical or emotional space with the person who has achieved the object of our desire. Whether it's one brother who always gets the lead in musicals while the other doesn't even get a part in the chorus, or whether it's a sister who gets into the Ivy League college that has rejected her twin, it is a challenge to figure out how to live with the person who has what we so unrequitedly desire. The more subtle challenge is how to live with ourselves at those moments when we feel life is so unfair.

Hannah's infertility illustrates the first thing that God acquires in this chapter: The power over birth. We're immediately tipped off that human beings do not control pregnancy and childbirth. Fertility is in the hands of God, and if we think we control our fertility, we're in for a shock. For those of us who scoff at this idea, just think of all the techniques we try to have a baby, and sometimes they work, and sometimes they just don't. Also think of the surprises: The years of infertility that lead us to believe that pregnancy is impossible, and then, after we've given up any belief in the possibility of pregnancy, the miracle happens.

In the biblical belief system, God is in control of pregnancy.

If God wants you to be pregnant, you will be, and if not, your womb is closed. We hear that God closed Hannah's womb, but we have no idea why. We struggle with this issue today as Hannah did so many years ago. We can be good, we can be kind, we can work hard, and bad things can happen to us. It feels absolutely unfair, and it happens anyways. We try so hard to control everything in our lives, and make the outcomes predictable, and so much of that is an illusion. So much is just out of our hands. When a brilliant teacher is diagnosed with a disease that takes away his ability to speak, when an adolescent volunteer is killed in a car crash on her way to building homes for the homeless, we all ask why this happens to these people, and none of us can come up with an answer. The challenge is how to cope with the unpredictable losses that we experience and use them to find greater meaning in life. And Hannah needed to figure out a way to meet that challenge.

So each year, Elkana, Hannah, Penina and Penina's children go to the holy place Shilo to worship, sacrifice to God and partake in the sacrificial meal. Elkana sees to it that Penina and each of her children receive portions of the sacrificial meal, and he also makes sure that Hannah receives a generous share. Even at that holy moment, when they connect with God through sacrifice, Hannah is reminded of her childlessness. One portion goes to her, while so many portions go to Penina to divide among her children. And Hannah watches this ritual, year after year, in painful silence.

This event—going up to Shilo, sacrificing to God, dealing out the portions to Hannah, Penina, and the children—happens every year. It is a predictable cycle, much like a woman's cycle, but with no pregnancy, only the reminder that cycles go on all around Hannah and she is excluded.

Not only does Elkana give Hannah a generous portion, but we are also told that he loves her. In a replay of the Leah-Rachel story (see Chapter 4), we again see the juxtaposition between the wife who has children and the wife who is loved by her husband. In Hannah's abject misery, we don't get any clue that she either is comforted by her husband's love, or that his favoritism might be painful to Penina. So self-absorbed is she in the sadness of her own loss that there is no indication that she can empathize with Penina's life in a loveless marriage. We often make the same mistake. When we covet another person's life, we often are blinded to their pain. Can a sibling who feels unattractive ever appreciate that her beautiful sister is unhappy because she believes that she is accepted only for her physical beauty?

We are told that Penina taunts Hannah about her childlessness. Perhaps Penina actually says hurtful words and makes insensitive statements. Perhaps she goads the silent, weeping Hannah to do something more with her life than wallow in self-pity.[2] Or perhaps she does neither. Anyone who has ever struggled with infertility knows that all one needs to do is see a mother with her children to feel taunted. A dear friend of mine felt taunted when I sent her a birth announcement. Like Hannah, my friend was silent. Years later, after she adopted a wonderful child, she told me that at the time, she thought I was cruel and insensitive for sending that announcement to her when she was trying unsuccessfully to conceive. How painful it is to always have to face what you long for and can't have! Hannah deals with her pain in silence and by not eating.

Biblical writers understood what psychologists have spent years trying to comprehend. When one is silent in the face of pain, when one is too disconnected from others to share the hurts, when one feels devalued and unable to address the devaluing, then one is at risk for psychological difficulties such as anorexia. After all, self-starvation reflects the internal emptiness that the anorexic feels and is a metaphor for the lack of sustenance in her life and relationships. Just as silence seems to scream out from within her, so the anorexic's thinness jumps out at everyone who looks at her, making her sense of invisibility visible to the world.[3]

Elkana tries to reach out to Hannah, but he seems perplexed by his beloved's sadness and refusal to eat. He doesn't understand why she remains unhappy enough to starve herself. After all, she is married to a man who loves her. He asks Hannah, "Am I not better to thee than ten sons?"[4] Hannah does not respond. Once again, she is silent.

But how does a woman respond to that question? How does she share her aloneness, her longing, her feelings of worthlessness, and her self-doubts with a man who loves her but already has children? Perhaps Elkana asks the wrong question.[5] His question supposes that his love for Hannah outweighs her desire for sons, but her anorexia belies his assumption. And, is it even realistic to assume that one relationship is enough to meet all our needs and deal with all our joy and pain? Furthermore, his question says nothing of Hannah's worth to him. He does not say, "I would rather have you than have sons." Those statements might communicate to Hannah that his love for her exceeds *his* desire for children; that he values her whether or not she has sons. But Elkana doesn't make this statement, nor could he. He already has sons. He has no idea what it would feel like to be childless, or son-less. Even more to the point, he has no idea what it is like to be a childless woman at a time when women are valued for their fertility. He has both the woman he loves and the children he desires. It would take an empathic leap for him to connect with Hannah's misery.

Perhaps what Elkana could have done was simply to hear Hannah's sorrow, much as Abraham needed to hear Sarah's pain (see Chapter 2). Perhaps Elkana needed to empathize with her plight, to share with her how difficult it must be for her to want a child so badly and not have one, and how painful for her to see other women around her giving birth as if it were easy. Hannah might not have felt better, but perhaps she would have felt more understood, less invisible, less alone. Perhaps she might even have eaten.

One of Liz's chief complaints was that her father would try to comfort her by telling her that she had a great husband, a nice home, and her health, and why couldn't she appreciate those blessings. Liz felt absolutely misunderstood.

Grief isn't about devaluing the blessings in our lives, it's about mourning that blessing that never came to be or that couldn't last. So, although Elkana is a kind and loving husband, his misunderstanding of Hannah and the pain she feels might have contributed to her silence. After all, at this point in the story, Hannah still has not uttered even a single word. She cries, she doesn't eat, and she is voiceless.

Yet, even given this critique, something in Elkana's words must have moved Hannah, because after the family finishes their meal, Hannah goes alone to the place of sacrifice at Shilo. We don't know whether his words offer her a bit of hope or whether his words push her over the edge of feeling misunderstood and unappreciated. Either way, she goes up to Shilo. There, in the place where people come to offer God what is valuable to them with the hope of making some connection with the Eternal One, Hannah offers her silent prayer and discovers her internal voice. This voice is a highly personal, deeply hidden one that we try and try to access and finally, if we're lucky, can sort out from all the internal noise. It is interesting that it is in God's place that Hannah could discover that private voice. And she does so in an unusual way. Hannah brings no animal, the usual object of value that one gives to God. She sacrifices no living creature. Instead, what she gives up to God is the self-protective silence that is both familiar but also keeps her in pain. That silence does have value, although it doesn't allow her to grow. It keeps her out of arguments, it keeps her from being publicly vulnerable, and it doesn't rock the boat with her beloved Elkana. But it also keeps her from knowing herself, connecting with God, and aspiring to anything better in her life. So, Hannah sacrifices her silence and she prays.

How remarkable! In this time of sacrifices, before the building and destruction of the Temple and the emergence of prayer as a way of connecting with God, Hannah prays. At a time of intermediaries when Levites are responsible for the sacrificial practices, Hannah directly calls to God. At a time when women's voices aren't heard in the sanctuaries and men are the priests, Hannah speaks straight to The Eternal.[6]

Hannah's prayer appears to be as much bargaining with God as praying to God. Hannah vows that if God gives her a son, she will give that son to God. At first reading, it makes little sense to us that Hannah would ask for a child and then give him away, or even that she would make a decision about her child's future before he is even born. Isn't it his life and his decision? If we love basketball, is it fair to commit our child to play basketball for the rest of her life before we know anything about her, her abilities, and her desires? However, before we leap to the conclusion that Hannah placed limitations on her son, perhaps we need to examine what it means to give a child to God.

In Torah, we see many examples of people who serve. Sometimes they serve God and sometimes they serve false gods. So, for example, the Children of Israel served Pharaoh, a false god, for many years. That type of service is considered bondage. We

144

were then told that God would free us from Pharaoh and take us out of Egypt so that we could serve God.[7] True freedom is defined as living in the service of God. Hannah understands that if she were to raise a child to be truly free, he had the possibility of being so only if he were dedicated to God. After all, we are always serving something or someone so that the ultimate question is whom we are serving and for what reason.[8] Serving God can open up a wide range of possibilities for us, if we could only understand what it means to serve God and why in our tradition, serving God is true freedom.

So, what does it mean to serve God? Since we are made in the image of God, when we serve God, we are the most ourselves that we can possibly be, as authentic as we can possibly be. To serve God is to find the best in ourselves and move along the path that allows us to actualize the best in ourselves. This child of Hannah's will not be silenced. This child will look deep inside and find the voice within and follow that voice. He will follow the path that is most true for him because his mother had vowed that he will serve God and thus not be detoured by false gods. In that service, Hannah's son is blessed with the possibility of truly knowing himself and following a road that is authentically his.

But what does Hannah know about motherhood that enables her to make that vow? On the one hand, Hannah knows very little about motherhood. She only knows that she is desperate to give birth to a son, but she never mentions any desire to parent a child. Initially at least, much of her focus is on demonstrating that she is capable of bearing a child, perhaps to silence her adversaries, perhaps to fulfill what society labels as her role, and perhaps because a "closed womb" can be understood as God's punitive action. Yet, if we look more closely, we can see a woman with a deep and complex understanding of motherhood. Most of us who become parents imagine our children growing up thinking, feeling, believing much of what we think, feel and believe. We may say that we want a child with a mind of his/her own, but usually there are some parameters for what we find acceptable difference. Many of us highly educated parents assume our children will go on to college and can't even begin to imagine alternative routes. It is a rare parent who can truly commit from the start to support her son on his most authentic path, regardless of what that path might be. We fight and we struggle, and ultimately, the lucky ones are able to come to terms with supporting our children's decisions. But usually it's after, and not prior to, the struggle. Hannah knows that just as pregnancy is not in our control, the inner passions of our children are not in our control. She knows that central to being a good parent is to respect our children's inner passions and to help them find a way to discover and actualize those desires. And, she knows to dedicate her child to God and not to herself.

When Hannah goes to pray, she walks past the priest, Eli, who is sitting by the gate. When Eli sees the distraught Hannah moving her mouth with fervor, he assumes she is drunk. Far from reflecting alcohol use, Hannah's lip movements are a sign of the inner conversation between her and God. When Eli accuses Hannah of drinking, we see a far different Hannah than the silent, embattled woman who refused to eat at her husband's table. Here instead is a woman with emerging voice. Instead of responding in silence to Eli's accusations, Hannah can now speak truth to power. To his accusation, she responds "No, my lord." What courage she has! When confronted by an authority figure, Hannah disputes his words and does not allow him to impose his ideas on her inner experience. Rashi, a great biblical scholar of the Middle Ages, tells us that Hannah said, "You are not my lord in this matter. There is no Holy Spirit in you or you'd know I'm not drunk."[9] Perhaps chastened by Hannah's ability to know herself and dispute his wrong impression of her, perhaps open to making amends when he recognizes that he is wrong, Eli then tells Hannah to go in peace and that he hopes that God will grant her petition.

Another reading of Eli's words could be that he told Hannah to "go to wholeness." This reading perhaps allows for a more insightful Eli. When Eli finds out that Hannah is not drunk, perhaps he is able to begin to understand how unhappy, fragmented, incomplete she had been feeling. Perhaps he even begins to see that prayer, this new communication with God, offers an opportunity to integrate the hurt, broken parts of ourselves. Perhaps Eli is hoping that through prayer, Hannah could begin her journey toward wholeness.

Through her prayer and her conversation with Eli, Hannah not only gains voice, but also defines what it means to have a voice: What Hannah gains is a knowledge of herself and what she needs, a connection with God that does not require an intermediary, and a belief that God can make her life right. Once Hannah is able to ask for what she needs and openly responds to someone who misunderstands her, she is able to eat and she is no longer sad. For Hannah, finding her private voice and daring to go public with it seems to counter both her anorexia and her depression.

What makes Hannah discover her voice? How does she begin to speak internally and then directly to Eli after such long silence? We can say that perhaps she was driven to that point by Penina's taunting or the presence of children in the household, except that she had been living in that situation for a long time. We can say she was inspired by being in Shilo, but she had gone up to Shilo every year. Perhaps just as we can't explain why unfair things happen to good people, we also can't quite explain the reversal of fortune. But, the acknowledgement that meaningful and wonderful life-altering moments are possible, albeit at times arbitrary, is our first glimpse at the meaning of Grace, the English equivalent of Hannah's name. It is at this moment, when Hannah can find a voice after long silence, when she can find connection with God after profound disconnection, that we see God's grace at work. Hannah's challenge becomes to hold that experience of grace and allow it to shape her life.

When I again looked at Liz's Christmas card, I could remember that time long ago when she told me that a major step in her recovery from anorexia took place when she recognized that she had to grieve the loss of the possibility for biological children, and then embrace the prospect of parenting adopted children. Just as with Hannah, the healing involved tears as well as prayer. Liz had to take an active role in finding out ways to proceed with adoption, much as Hannah had to actively go to Shilo and pray to God. And, she needed to find ways of responding to people like her aunt who hurt her each time they asked her when she was planning to have children. The decision to adopt, coupled with the decision to respond to insensitive comments, were defined by Liz as turning points in her life. In fact, Liz didn't starve herself or throw up the entire time that it took to adopt their first son in spite of the many frustrations and uncertainties along the way. Liz had a belief and a direction and a hope, and like Hannah, she actively pursued it.

So the seasons go by and Hannah gives birth to a son whom she names Shemuel, or Samuel. While his name literally means either "God heard" or "God's name," Hannah says that she named him Samuel because "I asked him of God."[10] This statement acknowledges that God is in control of fertility, that children are acquired through God, and as we know from Hannah's agreement, that God acquires the child (remember Elkana's name!). The words "I asked" also make it clear that Hannah has acquired a voice and uses that voice in connection with God. At the same time, it is telling that she names her son "God heard." Judy Jordan, a psychologist at the Jean Baker Miller Institute, talks about "listening each other into voice."[11] Feeling heard by God might have made it possible for Hannah to develop a voice that moved from a quiet, diffuse internal region through to her lips and then out to the larger world.

When it comes time for the yearly pilgrimage to Shilo, Hannah, now full of voice, refuses to go up until after she weans her son. While weaning in Torah can certainly be a physical event, there is also a symbolic understanding of weaning. When we think of nursing, we imagine a mother nourishing her child. The child is weaned when he has taken in enough physical, spiritual and emotional sustenance to now use what he has absorbed as he enters the larger world. Hannah could have nursed Samuel, just as Yocheved did with Moses (see Chapter 5), until she passed to him her wisdom, values, and sense of relationship. Perhaps once Samuel took in whatever he could from his relationship with his mother, he was ready to use that relational knowledge to discover himself in connection with God. So, first she had to nurse and wean him. Until she could do this thoroughly and completely, he was unprepared to be brought up to God. As if to underline the symbolic possibilities, we are told that when Samuel was brought up to God, he was a "naar" the Hebrew word for adolescent.

We as mothers and fathers nurse our children through childhood and adolescence. Our children internalize much of what we give to them, much of what was co-created in the relationship, and then we let them go. Letting them go doesn't assume a cut-off from relationship, but rather an integration of relationship that a child can carry with him or her throughout life.

When Hannah tells her husband that she and her son would not go with him on their annual pilgrimage, Elkana ben Yerucham, "God acquired, Son of he who is compassionate," lives up to his name. He replies to Hannah, "Do what is good in thy eyes. Tarry until thou hast weaned him."[12] Unlike his earlier interaction with Hannah, when he asked whether he was worth more than ten sons, here he listens to her, supports her plan, and does not insert himself into a scenario that is between Hannah, Samuel and God. He doesn't say, "Why don't you prefer to come with me? Don't you know that your company means more to me than this son?" Instead, as his name informs us, he knows that God already acquired his son, and he is living up to the rest of his name by being compassionate toward Hannah through supporting her decision about when to bring their son up to God.

Once Samuel is weaned, Hannah "took/raised him up with her," and we are left to grapple with what those words mean. Much earlier in Torah, God tells Abraham to "raise up your son as an 'olah'" (Genesis 22:2), a word that can mean "burnt offering" and/or "raise-up."[13] Abraham assumes that God means he should sacrifice Isaac, and so Abraham binds and is about to slaughter Isaac when a messenger of God intervenes and a ram is substituted for the boy.[14] Hannah's raising up of Samuel to God may lie in juxtaposition to Abraham's binding of Isaac. While Abraham understands "raise up" to mean bind and sacrifice, Hannah understands that raising up is a way of unbinding our children, of freeing them to be the most that they can be. Hannah understands that raising up means finding an opportune time to connect with God and show thanks to God. When she raises her child to God, he is free to form and define a relationship with God. Her raising-up is not through binding or sacrificing her son. As if to reinforce that point, Hannah slaughters a bull and brings the child to "my God," thus owning her relationship with God and making it clear that there should be no mistaking the difference between animal sacrifice and raising-up a child to God.

What a challenge to us as contemporary parents! How do we raise our children to God and not sacrifice them? How do we know when it's time to let them go--whether it's to that first day of kindergarten or off to college--and have the faith that we've given them enough to help them live their lives morally and meaningfully? Hannah, using a strong voice, tells Elkana when it is not the right time, and just as strongly, brings her child to Eli when the time feels right.

When Hannah brings her child to Eli, she again prays. This time her prayer is one of thanksgiving and rejoicing. A joyful Hannah, full of voice, emerges praising God with such eloquence that her prayer is called one of the two greatest poems in the Hebrew Bible.[15] Through this prayer, we discover that Hannah has learned the meaning of her name, Grace. It is a prayer that recognizes both how unjust the world can be, how sad and desolate and barren, and the possibility of reversals. She praises God with the grace of someone who knows the importance of taking psychological responsibility for living in spite of death, for gathering spiritual wealth in the midst of spiritual poverty, for voice instead of silence, for emotional fertility in spite of the barren times.

Hannah's prayer is also significant in what it can teach us about voice.[16] Up until this point, Hannah went from silence, to private voice, to interpersonal voice. Now, with this powerful song, Hannah develops her communal voice. This voice goes beyond her needs and the needs of her immediate family, and enters the sociopolitical world. Her prayer is a vision of a moral world, a transformation of a topsy-turvy world that can be put right again through God's grace.

Hannah herself recognizes her movement toward voice and praises God for "enlarging" her mouth.[17] Yet, even as she gains voice, Hannah is aware that voice is given to her to be used in connection with God. In the same breath that she thanks God for her salvation, she also recognizes that the gift of voice does not give her license to use it profanely. The more power she experiences through speaking up and being heard, the more Hannah recognizes that true power and knowledge is greater than any human and so there is no justification for arrogance. In fact, Hannah goes so far as to say that the wicked will be made dumb, without voice. She predicts that the wicked shall be silent in darkness. To Hannah, that silence, that lack of self-knowledge and connection that made it impossible for her to know herself or make herself known to others, is a curse. Wisely, she understands that people who do wicked things are disconnected from themselves and others, and that they are therefore without voice and "in the dark." Voice is a blessing--it moves us from lonely disconnection to relationship--and Hannah knows that it should not be taken for granted or misused.

Joyfully, Hannah sings that "the barren has born seven and she that has many children has become wretched." Some of our rabbis interpret her statement to mean that Hannah gave birth to more children while Penina's children died.[18] However, it is hard for me to imagine Hannah, who had just stated that voice should not be used haughtily, rejoicing in the death of her adversary's children. Possibly, Hannah instead recognizes that Elkana always loved her, and now that she also has children, the scales are tipped against the unloved, miserable Penina.

Further, the prayer also specifies that the barren bore seven, but Hannah ultimately gave birth to six children, leading me to wonder whether her statement is meant as metaphor. Seven in Torah is the number of creation. So, perhaps Hannah means that in connection with God, it is possible to find a creative life. Hannah's prayer recognizes that a connection with our deepest inner voice, with what some of us call God, can lead to the birth of creativity in someone who has felt empty while missing that connection can lead to misery even in someone who has been productive.

One of Hannah's most moving statements in her prayer is that "The Eternal kills and gives life; he brings down to the grave and he brings up." The order of the words, death before life, summarizes her belief that God gives us new chances when we feel the most despondent. Hannah recognizes that bad things do happen to all of us, that parts of us die as we move through life. However, that's only half of the equation. Just as throughout our lives we experience little deaths, small and large losses, tiny and profound griefs, we also experience that God gives us new life.

Several months after her partner died, Rachel said to me in wonder, "You wouldn't believe what happened today. I laughed. Who would have thought I could ever laugh again? But there I was with my friend, and we were having coffee, and she said something and I laughed. I was sitting drinking coffee, just like other people, and I laughed, just like other people. It was so amazing. For that moment, I was alive again."

There is a way to move from death, from endings, to new beginnings, new opportunities, new and ripe moments in time. We all know the feeling of being so sad or so scared and then one moment, one day, we find ourselves smiling, or we get curious about something. In that moment we capture a glimpse of the hope that there is not only death, but also life. And, in appreciating that larger picture, in seeing God in that larger picture, we begin anew the process of entering life with all its possibilities for new life, and for of course, new death.

Similarly, Hannah acknowledges that the Eternal "makes poor and makes rich. He raises up the poor out of the dust..." We don't know whether she is referring to financial, spiritual, or emotional poverty, and perhaps her ideas encompass all three. Astonishing changes of fortune happen in Hannah's vision. When we are feeling that we have no resources, that we are steeped in emotional and spiritual poverty, God provides us with an opening to come out of the dust. I remember a story I heard from an economically successful man who, before his immersion in Torah study, had felt spiritually poor, and couldn't even name his poverty. He knew that with all the comforts that money could buy, he was still feeling empty. He told of recognizing a desire for a connection with God, and paying attention to that desire. He now tells his story from a spiritually richer place, from the place of someone who was raised out of the dust, who was poor and made rich.

Through her prayer-song, Hannah moves from interpersonal voice to using her voice to shape a world vision. In this vision, connecting with God can lead to surprising reversals, whether one is speaking of fertility, death or poverty. In this new order, arrogant, power-over moves are toppled, they lead to misery, spiritual poverty, and emotional death. Recognition of a different order, one conducted by God, leads to the hope of creativity, emotional life, and spiritual wealth. And for those who don't turn, who maintain their arrogance? They are relegated to silence in darkness. That inability to make sense of oneself and one's relationships is the worst punishment that Hannah can imagine. In the world to which Hannah gives voice, a world in which "it is not by strength that man prevails," power is no longer defined as power over the meek, but rather as power to connect with God and live a moral life that is rich in hope and possibility.

So Liz, who for so long was silent, listened to her inner voice, spoke from her heart about her desire for children and realized her dream of being a mother. The voice that was so tentative when she initially grieved her infertility grew stronger as she began the adoption process, and even more clear in response to people who made unthinking comments to her and her children ("Where did he get blonde hair in this family of brunettes?" or "I'm sure you love him as much as you would if he were your real child"). Her own personal experience gave Liz the impetus to move beyond personal and interpersonal voice. Empowered by her experiences and in touch with her beliefs, she knew it was her responsibility to help change the larger society. So Liz began educational classes for parents, teachers and administrators and addressed many of the issues that are painful to adoptive families. Liz is now full of voice. The poor became rich, the dead alive.

Hannah, who was silent for so long, leaves Shilo with a vision of the world as it can and should be, and a vision of how she can and should be. In this vision, she understands the meaning of her name, Grace. In an unpredictable world, in a world where bad things happen without explanation, there is a God who raises the emotionally dead and the spiritually poor. And, because we are made in God's image, we too can live our lives led by grace, led by the inner knowing that even when things go wrong, there is still the larger picture of a world waiting to be set right.

And each year, Hannah returns to Shilo with a small coat for her son. When God sent Adam and Eve into the world, to take on the challenges of living a life worth living (see Chapter 1), God clothed them, symbolically protecting them from the harsh elements. Hannah does the same for Samuel. Not only is Samuel dressed in the priestly "efod" (robe), he also has a coat from his mother, a reminder of where he came from. While the efod separates him from others and designates him as a special member of the priestly class, the coat connects him with family and with all people, and reminds him of the pre-weaning knowledge he obtained from his mother. Just as Hannah prayed directly to God without priestly intervention, so the coat reminds her son that he can be a priest, but a priest is simply a human being who has to find his own path to God, and whose mother can try to clothe him against the elements that will attempt to stand in his way.

Notes

1. While the Tanach does not call Hannah a prophetess, Megillah 14a, *The Babylonian Talmud*, names her as one of seven prophetesses. Meg14b (*ibid*), Targum (see Harrington, D.J. and Saldarini, A.J. (1997). *The Aramaic Bible: Targum Jonathan of the Former Prophets*. Wilmington, DE: Michael Glazier, Inc.) and Zohar all agree that she is a prophetess because of her power of prayer and her prediction (in her song) that Saul will fall and David will rise. For more on this, see Cook, J.E. (1999) *Hannah's Desire, God's Design*. Journal for the Study of the Old Testament Supplement Series 282, Sheffield, England: Sheffield Academic Press.

2. Some rabbis say that Peninah provoked Hannah to pray (rather than "fret") so that Hannah would ask God for a child. [Pesikta Rabbati 43:8, Nemoy, L. and Simon, M. (ed.s) (1968). *Pesikta*. New Haven, CT:Yale Judaica Series,Yale University.]

3. For a further discussion of the social and psychological meanings of anorexia, see chapter 4 Mirkin, M. (ed) (1994). *Women in Context: Toward a Feminist Reconstruction of Psychotherapy*. NY, NY: Guilford Press.

4. First Book of Samuel 1:8.

5. Cynthia Ozick argues that Elkana made a revolutionary feminist statement because he says that Hannah has value as a person without motherhood

HANNAH

and that her value isn't governed by her biology. I have trouble with this interpretation since Elkana does not say that Hannah is more valuable to *him* than ten sons. Marcia Falk wonders what would have happened if Elkana did not try to talk Hannah out of her feelings but instead respected them. See their Chapters in Buchman, C. and Spiegel, C. (1994). *Out of the Garden.* NY: Fawcett Columbine.

6. Hannah calls God "The Lord of Hosts," and our rabbis have wondered why she named God in such a way. Hannah explained that the angels, or upper hosts, don't multiply or die, while the lower hosts, the life God created on earth, do both. Hannah then tells God that since she is meant to die, as are the lower hosts, she should also have children as is the function of the lower hosts (see Pesikta Rabbati 43:3). The Talmudic tractate Berakoth 31b instructs that Hannah reminded God that every part of our body has a purpose, so that if God put breasts on her for the purpose of nursing, then God should give her a son so she can nurse with those breasts. The Jerusalem Talmud comments on Hannah's way of praying, and says that even when one is silent, God hears the prayers. R. Yose bar Haninah explicates that Hannah teaches us how to pray: when she speaks in her heart, it means that she concentrated; only her lips moved so we're supposed to mouth prayers, and we should not pray when drunk!

7. See Exodus 4:23; "I am the Lord your God who brought you out of Egypt to be your God."

8. I would like to thank Rabbi Alan Ullman for teaching the distinction between service to God and service to false Gods.

9. The Talmud, Berakoth 31a-31b also states that Hannah chides and corrects Eli.

10. First Book of Samuel, 1:20. "I have asked him of Yahweh" is more closely translated as "Saul," the first King of Israel whom Samuel would later anoint. Some commentators believe that Saul's birth history was purposely wiped out by this use of his name. It is my belief that when Hannah acknowledges that she asked Yahweh for her child, she is both noting that childbirth is in God's control and not ours, and also acknowledging that she found her voice and was able to use it to ask God for this son. That asking is

157

so full of voice that it represents much of what I see as important in the story of Hannah.

11. Personal Communication. Also, Nelle Morton talks about "hearing each other into speech."

12. First Book of Samuel, 1:23. This can be thought of as juxtaposed to the Abraham-Sarah story (see Gen.16:6; also see Chapter 2). When Sarai felt belittled by Hagar, Avram told her to do with Hagar what was good in her eyes, a statement that might feel dismissive. Elkana is able to go further and connect with Hannah. He not only told her to do what she felt was right, but he told her not to bring the boy to God this season. He therefore confirmed Hannah's plan, a sign that he took her ideas seriously.

13. See *The Saperstein Edition of the Torah: With Rashi's Commentary.* The word "alah" and "olah" have the same root. "Alah" is first used in First Book of Samuel 1:3 to describe Elkana's going up to God each year to worship and to sacrifice (the word for sacrifice here is "lizboach;" going up is "alah"). The next time we see "alah" is when we are told that Hannah did not go up after she gave birth to Samuel but instead said that she would wait until after he was weaned (First Samuel 1:22), and finally we hear that she took him up with her after he was weaned. Each of these times, the word represents a "going up" or "raising up" to God, not a sacrifice.

14. Both Isaac and Samuel are called by the word "naar," or adolescent, perhaps pointing out yet another parallel between them.

15. Some see this prayer as a later addition to the Bible and perhaps Davidian in origin. However, even if it were added later, the placement of the prayer is brilliant because it allows us to see that movement from the personal to the personal/political.

16. Hannah prays: "O Lord of Hosts, if thou wilt indeed look on the affliction of thy handmaid, and remember me, and not forget thy handmaid, but wilt give to thy handmaid a man child, then I will give him to the Lord all the days of his life, and no razor shall come upon his head." First Book of Samuel 1:11.

17. First Book of Samuel 2:1.

18. The rabbis went into detail about this saying that two of Penina's chil-

dren died for every one of Hannah's that was born, until Penina begged Hannah to spare her last two children. The seven children would thus include Hannah's five plus Penina's two remaining children (Pesikta Rabbati 47:7).

8

RUTH, NAOMI AND BOAZ: FINDING
SUSTENANCE IN THE HOUSE OF BREAD

*"I WANT TO go home!" Devora's mother said as she sat rest-
lessly in the same chair in the same apartment that had been
hers for the past twenty-five years. Devora took her mother's
bony hand in hers, allowing herself to note its fragility, the
black and blue marks that appeared around protruding veins.
"I want to go home," the eighty-five-year-old begged again.
"Yes, mama," Devora responded, trying to superimpose the
mother that she knew atop the stranger that Goldie had
become. Instead, a rapid series of snapshots emblazoned
themselves on Devora's mind's eye. Snapshots of times when
her mother behaved strangely, and she attributed it to the
normal aging process; times when she had become so accus-
tomed to her mother's bizarre behavior that she didn't even
notice it. But now she was ready to notice it with her heart
and soul, not only with a mind that processed the word
"Alzheimer's." Her heart opened to her mother in a way it
hadn't all those months, maybe years, when she had still
questioned her mother's disease, when she confused herself
by trying to believe the well-meaning relatives who said her
mom was just a little forgetful, a bit ornery. Devora knew, and
with this knowing, came an openheartedness that took her by
surprise, that even gave her some small measure of comfort.
As Devora sat in the musty living room, holding the gnarled
hand of her mother, Ruth's words came back to her so unex-
pectedly, so powerfully, that tears gathered in her eyes as*

she allowed the words to move through her, bringing her com-
fort, washing away fear and allowing the future to unfold
without resisting its inevitability. "Entreat me not to leave you
or to return from following after you," Ruth says to her shat-
tered mother-in-law, "for wherever you go, I will go, and
where you lodge, I will lodge, your people shall be my people,
and your God, my God." As these words reverberated within
her, Devora saw a vision of her mother, younger, before this
illness ravaged her mind and she knew that she would not
leave her in the ravages of dementia, that she would do what-
ever she could to travel the road alongside her, a road that
her God would expect them to travel together.

When we read the Book of Ruth, we know from the start that
we are going to meet an amazing woman. After all, not only is Ruth
one of only two women in the Hebrew sacred writings called
Tanach[1] to have a book named after her, she is also the only convert
with that honor. Further, we read her story on the holiday of Sha-
vuot, the holiday that marks the giving of Torah to the Jewish people, as well as the festival that expresses gratitude for the harvest.
As we will see, perhaps the book of Ruth is read at this special time
because it parallels the story of the giving of the commandments.
In the first story, a covenant is created between God and people, a
covenant that involves the best of mutual love, commitment, and
obligation. In the book of Ruth, we see this covenant played out
between people; we see the holiness in everyday relationship. In
response to a surrounding society that can often be ruthless, this
book shows us what happens when we are instead Ruth-full.

In some ways, it is difficult to imagine how Ruth comes to
play such an important role in our text and our lives. After all, she
comes from a very problematic ancestry. Ruth is a Moabite, a
daughter of the tribe that turned us away when we were hungry and

thirsty during our wanderings in the wilderness.[2] This was the tribe
that unsuccessfully attempted to place a curse on our people. This
was the tribe that originated from incestuous relationships between
Abraham's nephew Lot and his daughter, thus its name "Moab,"
meaning "from the father."[3] Yet, out of this tribe was also born a
daughter who radiated with love, commitment, and purpose. Over
and over again in Torah we are told that our parents, our religion,
our ancestry, cannot excuse us from our obligation to become the
best people we are capable of becoming. In fact, we all know that
difficult experiences can inspire some people to try to do things differently and help to repair the world. In the Kabalistic (Jewish mys-
tical) tradition, there is an idea that divine sparks of goodness are
entrapped in shells of evil.[4] People who are righteous penetrate the
evil to rescue the divine sparks. So, even if Moabites were seen as
evil, there was a righteous person trapped in that land.

The story begins during the period of Judges; a chaotic
period when Israel was not governed by kings, prophets, or
divinely inspired leaders. We find out that during this chaotic time,
there was a famine in Bethlehem, which can be translated as the
House of Bread. How can there possibly be a famine in a house full
of bread? What kind of famine? And, more to the point, how do we
deal with that famine?

I would suggest that bread here represents emotional as well
as physical sustenance, and that there are times when we all experience famine in our House of Bread. When people feel desolate,
when we are isolated and disconnected, we can be surrounded by
emotional nurturance and yet not be able to take in any of that caring. One of the biggest challenges during our lowest times is to recognize all the possible sustenance that surrounds us, and then to
begin the process of experiencing it as sustenance.

Two inhabitants of Bethlehem, Elimelech and Naomi, along

with their sons Mahlon and Kilyon, experience this famine. They deal with it by leaving the House of Bread and moving to Moab. Here we see a huge mistake that will take a tremendous toll on the family: They leave the House of Bread, the place where sustenance that they cannot recognize awaits them, to go to Moab, a land that denies bread. How could they possibly hope to find emotional sustenance by leaving the source of bread to move to a place that withholds it? And yet, we know of so many people who do that, who are hurting so badly that they assume it's their surroundings that cause the suffering, and so they leave the place of potential healing and find themselves suffering somewhere else.

Miguel was inconsolable after the sudden death of his wife whose car was hit by a drunk driver. Friends and neighbors surrounded him and eight-year old Lucy, trying to find words of comfort, bringing offerings of food. The words were meaningless to the bereft Miguel who experienced them as insufficient and shallow. The faces irritated him—the looks of sadness and pity on the faces of people who would soon leave him to enter the healthy arms of someone they loved. He couldn't bear to look at the food that rarely resembled the delicately spiced dishes that were his wife's specialty. So Miguel decided to move, to leave this barren land and begin anew. But then there were Lucy's tears. Lucy, who didn't want to leave her friends and teachers and familiar school; who didn't want to leave the smell of her mother that still lingered in the closet that remained full in her room. Yet, if Miguel believed that he could leave their sorrow in the old saltbox house, he would take Lucy from the place where both of them might be able to find sustenance.

As we would imagine, Elimelech dies in Moab.[5] Unable to find sustenance where it is available and certainly not able to find it where it is not available, Elimelech cannot emotionally survive. Interestingly, Elimelech's name means "My God is King." Had he been able to access the part of himself that understood his name, he would have returned to the House of Bread. Bethlehem is part of the Promised Land, the land where God is King, the land that Elimelech's name beckons him toward. That sounds very abstract, but we live through this in our own lives. If we can allow ourselves to live in Bethlehem, to access the loving, caring relationships that surround us, or place ourselves in situations where there is potential for emotional sustenance, we often find fulfillment. But, if we ignore or battle our inner voice, and isolate ourselves from our sustenance, we're in for trouble. So, if Elimelech doesn't recognize that his essence is "God is King," he can't recognize that he should be living in God's land and he deserts the land.

So Elimelech dies, and his wife Naomi, whose name means pleasantness, is left with her two sons, whose names can be translated as "sickly" (Mahlon) and "comes to an early end" (Kilyon). How can a parent give children such strange and upsetting names? I believe Torah is arguing that it is our behavior that names our children. Elimelech and Naomi couldn't find the bread in the House of Bread, couldn't recognize the nourishment and sustenance that surrounded them. And they left. They left their community, separated themselves from the possibility of sustenance, and separated their children from those who could sustain them until their parents could once again find bread. When we as parents are feeling empty, when we refuse help and isolate ourselves from our community, we are also severing our children from those very people who could keep them going during our tough times. Mahlon and Kilyon give us two models of how children can react to living in isolated, non-nourishing situations. Like Kilyon, some children come to an early end: their childhoods end prematurely. I know a sixteen-year-old who once said to me, "Of course I can take care of myself. But, at sixteen, I shouldn't have to." She was thrust into adulthood, leaving her unfinished childhood behind. On the other hand, there are children who are like Mahlon. These children, when they perceive that their parents are emotionally unavailable and when they are isolated from a supportive community, become more sickly. These are the children who unconsciously use the strategy of illness—perhaps frequently claiming to be too ill to go to school, or cutting themselves, or refusing to eat, or developing physical pain—in response to the sense of isolation and hopelessness. Not every child in this situation will end up being sickly or coming to an early end, but the Torah is possibly waving a red flag, warning us to think carefully about leaving what can nourish us because our choices influence how our children understand and live their lives.

We are told that while their parents sojourned in Moab, Mahlon and Kilyon dwelled there.[6] Their sons complete the disconnection that their parents began. If Mahlon and Kilyon are dwelling in Moab, then they have no intention of returning to the House of Bread. Disconnected from their community, their God, and their sustenance, they live out their lives in self-imposed exile. During this time, they marry Ruth and Orpah, both Moabite women, and ten years after the death of their father, they too die.

After the death of her sons, we finally hear something about Naomi. The typical translation is that Naomi was bereft of her two sons and her husband. However, the Hebrew can be understood more intensively as "saturated with grief." We hear that Naomi feels like the leftovers after a meal offering. According to Zornberg, those leftovers are inessential, the residual, the husk.[7] Her sons are referred to with the word used for young children, which further taps into the sense of a mother's grief after such an overwhelming loss. This once pleasant woman, who I imagine made the best out of a miserable situation in Moab, and then had to mourn the premature loss of her husband, is now faced with the worst imaginable tragedy—she outlives her sons. And now she feels completely empty, a useless, worthless husk. If she once were hungry in the House of Bread, now we get the sense that she doesn't even have a hunger, that hunger still represents life and can be an energizing force, motivating us to partake in more of what life can offer. She is beyond hunger. She is a human form with nothing left inside.

And yet, in spite of the tragedy, in spite of her grief, in spite of her emptiness, there is something about Naomi that doesn't totally give up. Caught in the bleakness of Moab and the darkness of her tragic life, Naomi still somehow hears that God visited Bethlehem and there is bread in her native land. By noticing that God visits people who are experiencing famine in the land of bread, she is finally seeing the sustenance that was there all along. Just as God visits a parched Hagar and she is able to see a sustaining well that she couldn't see earlier (see Chapter 2), so God also visits the famished House of Bread and the people who are aware of this visit are sustained by the bread that was there all along. So, in spite of her grief and in spite of her depression, Naomi raises herself up to return home. Sometimes, we have to take action before something improves, even if we're not totally convinced that things will get better.

The action that Naomi takes is not simply raising herself up. It's raising herself up in order to return. The Hebrew root of the verb "to return" is the same as the root of "Teshuva." Teshuva is an act of turning until we are facing away from what has been harmful to us and toward what is growth-sustaining. So Naomi is about to "re-turn," to turn again, away from the destructiveness of the years in Moab and toward the land that she once rejected.[8]

While Naomi has the amazing courage to begin her healing journey, she remains disconnected from her people and her sustenance at this point in the story. She reports that God visited "His" people; she doesn't say "my people" although she is referring to the residents of Bethlehem. Naomi is estranged from God and community and will be restored by human acts. The drama that unfolds is a story of the human dedication that makes this restoration possible.

As Naomi leaves Moab, both her daughters-in-law accompany her. By the time they get to the crossroads, Naomi calls them "daughters" but advises them to return to their mother's house. Perhaps Naomi had been the spiritual mother of these women, but recognizes that she is an empty shell and wants something better for the children she loves. Perhaps Naomi recognizes that while she has loving feelings for these younger women, they would be better off staying in Moab where they could remarry in their own community. After all, Israelites were commanded in Torah not to marry Moabites. Or, perhaps Naomi knows all too well the grief of a mother who lost her children, and cannot subject Orpah's and Ruth's mothers to that despair. In any case, she encourages both women to return home to their mothers, and blesses them with God's "chesed."

Chesed is a central word in this story. Chesed is the loving kindness that makes healing and redemption possible. It is the loving kindness beyond anything we have the right to expect or could ever imagine asking for. It is this generosity of spirit that Naomi hopes God will extend toward Ruth and Orpah. Yet, the God of the Ruth story is not a proactive God. No seas part in this book, no plagues strike upon the order of the Almighty. So, without an interventionist God, how can God's chesed be manifested? I believe the book of Ruth is a powerful demonstration that God's chesed is evidenced by human actions. Our own kindness-beyond-kindness, loving-beyond-loving, is a reflection of God's chesed, God's loving-kindness. This is a book that plants the responsibility for God's healing love squarely on our human shoulders.

As Naomi kissed her daughters-in-law goodbye, they wailed and cried. How could they leave Naomi? How could they leave Pleasantness? In spite of the tragedy, they lived with Pleasantness and now she wants them to leave. With compassion that one would not expect from an empty husk of a woman, Naomi attempts to explain to them why it is in their best interests to leave her. After all, she cannot provide them with another son to wed. Even worse, she believes that the hand of God is against her, so in a sense they are at risk if they stay with her, and if she has any desire left, it's for them to have a life full of the loving kindness that they showed to her sons and to her.

As Naomi tells Ruth and Orpah to return home, she kisses them. People are rarely kissed in Torah. With tears in his eyes, Jacob kisses his newly-met future wife, Rachel. These are kisses of human transformation. Perhaps Naomi's kiss isn't a goodbye kiss, but a kiss that reminds Ruth of all the openings possible when there is love and friendship, a kiss that transforms Ruth and opens her life in ways she never dreamed possible.

Crying, Orpah turns back. She is the obedient daughter-in-law, the one convinced by Naomi's tearful pleading. Although our tradition is sometimes harsh on Orpah,[9] one can hardly blame the Moabite for returning to her mother and her community and what is familiar to her.

But Ruth doesn't turn away. Ruth clings to Naomi as if her life depends on it, and in fact, her life does. There are times when we join a person who is in need, and it appears as if we're helping them with no benefit to ourselves. Ruth shows us that this simply isn't true. Clinging to Naomi will be her salvation as well as

Naomi's. After all, Ruth is clinging to pleasantness. In an important Hebrew prayer[10] we sing that Torah is our tree of life, that her ways are pleasant, and all who cling to her find wholeness. In a story where humans represent qualities that are holy, Ruth has to cling to Naomi/Pleasantness in order to become more whole, more complete.

So Ruth says to her mother-in-law those famous, beautiful, poetic lines: "Entreat me not to leave you, or to return from following after you: for wherever you go, I will go; and where you lodge, I will lodge; your people shall be my people, and your God my God; where you die, I will die, and there will I be buried."[11] My dear friend and colleague Mona Fishbane[12] writes that "entreat me not" can also be translated as "hurt me not," with the recognition that separating from Naomi would be damaging to Ruth and that what appears to be altruistic behavior is an inner knowledge that this relationship is redemptive. By clinging to pleasantness, Ruth develops the ability to make it through the hard times. Perhaps if Elimelech had clung to the pleasantness that surrounded him in the House of Bread, and didn't leave when the going got rough, he too could have survived.

Devora understands this. So many people told her that she's being a "saint" by emotionally supporting and arranging care for her mother. But Devora knew that it had nothing to do with sainthood, and everything to do with her soul. She knew that she was being stretched in ways that she never believed possible, and by clinging to pleasantness as she helped her mother, she was growing more and more into the type of person she wanted to become, a person who could be a blessing, who could impact the world with one more spark of kindness, and who could feel greater satisfaction with life as a result.

Who is this Ruth, this woman who could leave all that she knows to go with a husk, a shell, of a human being to a land she does not know? Ruth's name has been linked to many meanings. It is sometimes seen as coming from the word "Ravah," meaning saturate or irrigate with water.[13] Here, Ruth is seen as someone who can emotionally fill another, who can offer spiritual sustenance. Ruth's name has also been connected with "ra-ah," to see. She is a woman of vision, who can look beyond the moment, who knows that "pleasantness" needs to be followed even though it cannot be experienced as such at every moment, who can envision connection with another as life-giving. Finally, Ruth's name is also linked with the word "re-ut," or friendship. And what a paragon of friendship she is! Through her way of living her life, Ruth defines friendship for us as staying in relationship through the hard times as well as the good times, being able to both receive and give, recognizing that giving is also a way of helping ourselves.

Ruth also takes on the stature of our first foreparents. Like Abraham and Rebecca (see Chapters 2 and 3), she leaves her parent's house, her kin, and her country to go to a new land. While God sent Abraham to the land, and Rebecca leaves for that land at the bequest of Abraham's servant, Ruth takes it upon herself to go to the land of the covenant. No anthropomorphized God tells her to go. She receives none of Abraham's promises of reward. In this story, a person trusts a relationship with another person enough to take that step into the unknown. But Ruth's story not only is reminiscent of Abraham and Rebecca. Ruth also replays the story of the Exodus. The holiness of Ruth's story comes from the covenant between people, and parallels our story of leaving Egypt, entering a covenant at Sinai, and entering the Promised Land. This time, Ruth enters a covenant with Naomi after they leave Moab and have approached the wilderness. Her words echo the long ago awesome moment at Sinai when we said "You are our God and we are your people," just as Ruth now says, "Your people are my people and your God my God." In this wilderness, in the middle of nowhere on the way to somewhere, Ruth accepts God, and moves forward with her beloved friend toward the Promised Land.

Naomi has nothing to say in response. She can offer Ruth no words of encouragement, not even any hope. The future is fraught with danger. Naomi herself believes she can offer nothing to Ruth. Will anybody in Judah accept a Moabite woman in their midst? Will she always be an outcast, a stranger? Is this unknown better for Ruth than the known of Moab? Further, if Naomi once thought that there was no sustenance in Judah, what will she find there when she returns from abandoning her homeland? And so they journeyed in silence toward the Promised Land.

Devora's mother didn't seem to notice that her daughter empathically saw to it that she was well cared for, ate her favorite foods, slept in a clean and familiar environment. But Devora, perhaps for the first time in her life, was not looking for Goldie's approval. Being with her, opening her heart to her, making it possible for her to live out her days in dignity, was a more internally expansive experience for Devora than all the praise her mother could have bestowed, were she able to bestow it.

As the depressed, grieving widow and her bereaved daughter-in-law are seen approaching Bethlehem, the women of the city are in a panicked frenzy.[14] "Is this Naomi?" they ask incredulously. Their reaction is not lost on Naomi. She responds to them that her name is no longer Naomi, or pleasantness, but Mara, bitterness. She shares that she left Bethlehem "full," and returned empty. She shares that God has dealt bitterly with her, and that El Shaddai, the

God whose name may come from the word breast, whom we can associate with nurturing babies, returned her empty, childless, with a womb that cannot produce more babies. How painfully ironic! Naomi, because she believed there was a famine in the House of Bread and felt so empty, left Bethlehem to settle in Moab. It was only years later, when she had lost everything that mattered to her, that she recognized that perhaps she was full in the House of Bread after all, and that the emptiness she now feels is perhaps tinged with overwhelming regret for not appreciating her blessings when her husband and children were alive. At this moment, she understandably feels that even God has turned against her and that she has nothing.

In her sorrow, Naomi cannot see that she is moving toward repeating her mistake from years ago. Just as she had what she needed back then, but didn't recognize it, so now she has Ruth and does not feel, let alone acknowledge, the meaningfulness of that relationship. She will feel empty, abandoned even by God, until she can let in the friendship, vision, and the saturation of sustenance that are Ruth. At this moment, Ruth is spoken of as a Moabite stranger, as a daughter-in-law, but not with the intimacy of the word "daughter." For the time being, Naomi is keeping Ruth, her salvation, at a distance.

So the women return to Bethlehem at the beginning of the barley harvest, at a time when everything surrounding them is full of growth, life and sustenance. Perhaps there is hope that their emptiness will be filled. And now the stage is set for our mourning characters to begin healing. They are surrounded by all that they need, and their challenge is to find a way of recognizing that and taking it in.

The rest of the story reads almost like a fairy tale, perhaps the only biblical narrative in which the main characters appear to be perfect heroes who live happily ever after. It is so unlike Torah to have protagonists who are so good because we can learn so much more from fallible beings with whom we can identify. I prefer to see the final chapters of this book as a parable; the story of what happens when we live in the Land in the way God envisioned it for us. We are told in Torah that if we follow God's teachings, we will live long in the land. The Land can be understood as a psychological space in which we live our lives as a blessing, open ourselves to receive blessings, and extend ourselves to others with the same loving kindness that we feel from God. If we are capable of this type of life, the rewards are measureless, and hence the fairy tale ending.

But, protagonists in fairytales first have to respond to their difficult situation before they can live happily ever after. Ruth realizes from the beginning that she will need to actively seek sustenance in her new home, and asks Naomi's permission to glean corn from the fields. The law is that the reapers gather whatever they can, but whatever falls can be taken by people in need who follow behind the reapers. Naomi, too old to glean from the fields herself, perhaps understands that seeking after sustenance is a step toward healing, and she replies, "Go my daughter." At that moment, in spite of everything, Naomi has the emotional lucidity to recognize and acknowledge the true closeness of her relationship with Ruth. At that moment, Ruth is her daughter and she is not empty.

In a flurry of activity reminiscent of Rebecca (see Chapter 3), Ruth quickly goes to the fields and begins gathering food. As fortune (or God) would have it, part of the field is owned by Naomi's relative, Boaz. The biblical narrator describes Boaz as a great man of valor from the family of God is My King. Unlike Elimelech, however, Boaz did not leave Bethlehem. He stayed in the land, was nurtured by it, and is a successful landowner whose fields are ripe with corn.

Boaz's name means "In him is strength," and so we are able to get an insight into what qualities of strength are revered in the Bible. This is not the strength of a military leader; it is not about overpowering or making buildings crumble. The strength we find in Boaz is strength of character and faith, it is the ability to live life with chesed, the quiet strength of knowing that we find bread when we serve God and that we serve God by enacting the sacred covenant here on earth. When Boaz arrives at the fields, his first words to the workers are "The Eternal be with you," and they answer, "The Eternal bless you." In Boaz's eyes, this is God's field, and its ripeness and richness is God's blessing. And we, who have followed the tragedy of Naomi, certainly understand what a blessing it is to recognize bread when it surrounds you and to recognize God's hand in sustenance and fulfillment.

When Boaz notices and inquires after Ruth, his servant answers that she is a Moabite who came back with Naomi, asked to glean and gather in this field, and worked very hard all day. While the servant is able to recognize Ruth's dedication to gathering sustenance, he considers Ruth a stranger, a Moabite, an enemy of Israel. Boaz responds very differently. He calls Ruth to him and identifies her as his daughter. She is not a stranger, an enemy, a Moabite. Our introduction to biblical strength, as personified by Boaz, is openhearted inclusion of all people as children of God.

Boaz then introduces Ruth to his fields, perhaps a metaphor for the spiritual Promised Land. He tells her to stay on this land[15]— and Ruth well knows what happens when one abandons the land. He recognizes that she thirsts for more out of life, and encourages her to drink. He provides her with friends, with women who can perhaps give to her in some of the ways that she gave to Naomi. Perhaps he is even offering her the hope of marriage: it is a typical biblical courting scene for men and women to meet around a well, and here Boaz tells Ruth to drink the water that the men draw for her.

But Ruth, who is called a stranger by Boaz's servant, who may still feel like a stranger internally, who experiences life as hard and friendship as unreciprocated, can't help but ask Boaz why he has shown her such grace. And we too wonder why Boaz shows such kindness to a stranger. Perhaps Boaz remembers his forefather Abraham, Abraham who was told to take himself from his father's house and from the land of his birth, and go to a land that he does not know. Perhaps he sees the connection between this holy man and Ruth, and replies that he has heard of what Ruth has done, that she "hast left thy father and thy mother, and the land of thy birth, and art come to a people whom thou knewest not before. The Lord recompense thy deed."[16] Then Boaz takes it even further and tells Ruth, "may a full reward be given thee by the Eternal God of Israel under whose wings thou art come to take refuge." His blessing hearkens back to Sinai, when we are told that God carries us under eagle's wings. Just as Ruth's behavior toward Naomi was a human-to-human replay of the God-to-human covenant at Sinai, so Boaz now also brings up images of the holy covenant. This is one large circle of "chesed," of loving kindness beyond our wildest hopes. As God gives to us so we give to each other and so make it possible to receive more from God. It therefore comes as no surprise that Boaz would call Ruth his daughter. Perhaps part of Boaz's strength is that when he sees something holy, he recognizes it, and claims it as his kin.

Boaz, in another act of chesed, goes beyond allowing Ruth to glean in his fields and drink when she is thirsty. He also decides to feed her, again hearkening back to our ancestor Abraham who fed the strangers. Perhaps since both Boaz and Ruth are compared to Abraham, we are being told that the two of them are soul mates, both spiritual children of our forefather. Unlike Elimelech who, according to Midrash, was not hospitable to others[17]—and perhaps as a result could not experience the redemptive nature of being part of a community—Boaz takes responsibility for the physical and spiritual needs of a stranger. He even warns his workers to be respectful of Ruth, and commands them to drop some of what they have picked so that Ruth will be able to gather it. Just as Ruth did with Naomi, Boaz shows Ruth chesed in a frightening world. And, bathed in Boaz's chesed, Ruth eats and is satisfied.

In this simple scene, a scene between a kind man, a loving stranger, and the land, we see played out the Commandments written in Deuteronomy 8:3-11: "...man does not live by bread only, but by every word that proceeds out of the mouth of the Lord does man live...Therefore thou shalt keep the commandments of the Lord thy God, to walk in his ways and to fear him. For the Lord thy God brings thee into a good land, a land of water courses, of wheat, and barley...a land in which thou shalt eat bread without scarceness...When thou has eaten and art replete, then thou shalt bless the Eternal thy God for the good land which he has given thee." Boaz and Ruth can experience fullness in the House of Bread, both physically and spiritually, because of their chesed, of their willingness to truly be there for another human being. They bless the eternal not only with words, but with how they live their lives.

At the end of the day, Ruth returns to Naomi, saturated with spiritual and physical food, and gives the rest of what she gleaned to her mother-in-law. And here is our first glimpse of Naomi's redemption. Naomi said that she came back to Bethlehem empty, but now she notices and accepts food from Ruth, food that was obtained in the House of Bread. When Ruth tells her that the field belongs to Boaz, Naomi can see God's hand in her redemption as well as in Ruth's. Boaz is her relative! Maybe she does have something to offer her daughter-in-law! With insightful discovery, Naomi responds, "Blessed is the Eternal one whose steadfast love is not left off to the living or dead." Naomi recognizes that even when she feels dead, God can still be there for her. Perhaps it wasn't God after all who made her empty! Perhaps instead it is God who can be with her through her emptiness and as she makes her way up toward life. This is the first time in this book that Naomi offers a blessing, and as we have seen from Boaz and Ruth, the more we bless, the more we are blessed.

Naomi tells Ruth that Boaz is close kin to "us," not simply to Naomi, thus again opening herself to connection with Ruth.[18] Then, very briefly, Ruth says something that could derail their path toward salvation. Ruth, now referred to as a Moabite, says that Boaz wants her to stay close to the young men, although Boaz in actuality told her something very different: He requested that she stay with the women. Instead of questioning Ruth's veracity, Naomi continues on the road toward salvation by calling Ruth her daughter and instructing her to stay with the women. Just as Ruth was about to move off track, Naomi, who now recognizes God's presence and is able to again give blessings, sweeps her back to the right path and does so not by reprimanding her but by drawing her closer, by referring to her as daughter.

Once Naomi is able to recognize God's unwavering love, she is again able to act in God's image and radiate that steadfast love. She now has a plan for Ruth. She tells Ruth to wash and anoint herself, an ambiguous instruction that could be understood as sexually provocative or as a ritual immersion or perhaps both. Naomi also tells Ruth to get dressed, and return to the field where Boaz and other men are sleeping on the threshing room floor. Naomi instructs Ruth to keep her identity hidden until Boaz finishes eating and drinking and he lies down. Then, Ruth is told to go in to the threshing room floor, uncover his feet, lie down, and listen to Boaz's instructions.

What is Naomi thinking as she gives these orders to Ruth? Is she asking Ruth to seduce Boaz, even to prostitute herself? After all, uncovering someone's feet at that time had sexual as well as transactional meaning.[19] Further, women in Torah are usually expected to stay in, not go out. Dina's rape was explained by the rabbis as being a result of her going out of the tents.[20] And, to make it even more dangerous, Naomi tells Ruth to listen to what Boaz tells her to do.

While this is certainly a risky plan, we have to remember that the two central characters are Boaz and Ruth, both capable of demonstrating chesed and of living God's covenant in their human world. So, Ruth obeys Naomi, waits until Boaz eats and drinks and lies down before she enters the threshing area and lies down at his feet. How does Ruth feel as she awaits Boaz's awakening? We don't know. We do know that at midnight, that moment when a new day is about to begin, Boaz wakes up and asks Ruth who she is. To understand some of the profundity of his question, we need to revisit his history. Tamar, one of Boaz's ancestors, was married to Judah's son. When Judah's son died, Tamar married his next son, who also died. Fearing that his youngest son would perish if he married Tamar, Judah withheld him from Tamar and did not proceed with the Levirite marriage, a tradition in which a brother is required to marry his brother's widow. A wronged Tamar, in an attempt to show Judah his errors and give him an opportunity for redemption not only from this act but for others in his past, disguised herself and slept with him. When she became pregnant and he accused her of wanton acts, she revealed that he was the father of the baby. Judah recognized the error of his ways and married

Tamar. So, as Boaz awakens in the dark, and a perhaps unrecognized woman is at his feet, he might wonder who she is on many levels. Is she sent to show him that he is perpetuating some wrong that needs to be corrected? Is she sent to lure him into transgression or to redeem him? Is she playing Tamar to his Judah? Who is she?

Or, perhaps Boaz does recognize Ruth, and perhaps he is asking her a biblically profound question. As Isaac once asked his floundering son Jacob, Boaz now asks Ruth, "Who are you?" Unflinching, Ruth answers with the profound knowledge of a woman who knows exactly who she is. "I am Ruth/vision/friendship/saturation, your handmaid; spread therefore thy skirt over thy handmaid; for thou are a near kinsman." Some commentators have explained that spreading one's skirt is an intent to marry.[21] However, "cheenafechah," which is translated to be "your skirt" can also be "your wings." When she tells Boaz to spread his wings over her, she might be offering a subtle reminder to Boaz that he previously told her to take refuge under God's wings. Since this is a story where people, not God, are proactive, then if Boaz were to act in the image of God, he needs to provide that refuge for Ruth. She is asking him to do this through his chesed rather than through any required sense of responsibility. She reminds him that he's a near relative, perhaps suggesting a Levirite marriage. However, Boaz is not a brother to Ruth's husband, at least not in the legal sense of the word, so he has no legal obligation to marry Ruth. Ruth, an expert in chesed, might be reminding him that chesed isn't about following the letter of the law. Ruth holds Boaz to a higher standard, to the standard of God's chesed, a standard that makes him responsible for Ruth's well being because we humans happen to be responsible for each other. Predictably and yet remarkably, Boaz responds lovingly to Ruth.

Boaz is moved by what he understands as Ruth's chesed, her

loving kindness beyond loving kindness. But why would he think Ruth's veiled proposal is yet another example of chesed, and even greater chesed than any previous act of hers? Perhaps just as Tamar gave Judah the opportunity for redemption, so Ruth gives Boaz a chance to live a life of even greater chesed than he had ever before experienced. Or perhaps she opened to an elderly Boaz the possibility of love and family that had eluded him throughout his life and certainly no longer seemed likely in his old age. Or, perhaps the chance to love Ruth, a woman he calls kind and virtuous, is redemptive. After all, when we give of ourselves, not only are we helping somebody else but we are also opening ourselves up to greater meaning in our own lives. Perhaps now Boaz can live up to his name, the name "In him is strength," the strength to recognize a woman who is as virtuous as he is, and to hold on to her as she did with Naomi.

Boaz tells Ruth that she can spend the night with him. Had he sent her home, she would have been at risk—she would have had to walk through the fields alone at night, and could have been accosted by one of the less ethical workers. By providing her with shelter for the night, he is protecting her. But, unlike Judah, Boaz does not make any sexual overtures toward her.[22] He also gives her more than enough barley to take care of Naomi and herself, and Ruth leaves before anybody can recognize her.

Upon returning home, Ruth is greeted by the now familiar "Who are you, my daughter." If Naomi could call Ruth her daughter, then why does she ask "who are you?" This is another example of the classical biblical statement about self-awareness. The Ruth who left the night before is not necessarily the same Ruth who returned the next morning. In the intervening hours, she experienced a man acting in the image of God, a man of chesed. She experienced her own voice and self-conviction, which she communicated in a subtle way that gave Boaz an out had he not wanted to marry her or take care of her. She made her own decisions in spite of Naomi's admonishment to do as Boaz says. She arrived a woman with a tenuous future, and left a woman whose future was assured. Ruth shared her experiences with her mother-in-law, and in her kindness, even embellished on Boaz's good nature. Not only did she acknowledge Boaz for giving her the barley, but she also credited him with saying that she should not go empty-handed to her mother-in-law!

In the meantime, Boaz has to deal with an obstacle that could stand in the way of his marriage to Ruth. There is another kinsman who is a closer relation to Ruth than Boaz. Boaz therefore has to see if this kinsman will choose to marry Ruth before he can commit to her. Boaz tells his kinsman that the relative has the opportunity to buy land from Naomi and Ruth, a Moabite, the wife of the dead. This is an interesting description of someone whom the night before Boaz calls his daughter. Perhaps again harkening back to the story of his foreparent, Judah, Boaz plays to the fear that some people have of marrying a widow. To make Ruth even less appealing to his competitor, Boaz emphasizes that she is a Moabite, of a tribe hated and feared by many Hebrews. The kinsman immediately sees Ruth as someone who brings bad luck, and refuses to redeem the land from her, thus making it possible for Boaz to marry Ruth.

As if confirming the subplot that runs throughout the story of Ruth and Boaz, the neighbors who witness Boaz's commitment to marry Ruth wish that his house would be like the house of Perez, son of Tamar and Judah. The people of Bethlehem also wish that Ruth would be like Leah and Rachel, the two foremothers who birthed eight of the Tribes of Israel. These foremothers (see Chapter 4) were able to stay in what must have felt like an impossible struggle until it was resolved. The hope of the women of Bethlehem was that Ruth, too, would not leave a struggle. If there were again a famine in the House of Bread, Ruth would stay and see it through.

In the Book of Ruth, God tends not to be proactive. Instead, people take on the chesed that we often attribute to God. Early on, God visits Bethlehem and then we do not hear of the active presence of God until the closing of the story when two people who have acted in God's image are blessed with a child. The impact of the birth of this child is not lost on the women of Bethlehem. They comment that God didn't leave Naomi without a redeemer. Naomi, who left Bethlehem full and didn't know it, and came back feeling empty in spite of Ruth's love, is now redeemed. She, who was a husk of a woman, now has a present and a future. She has a loving daughter and son-in-law and now, miracle of miracles, she also has a grandson. This is the world she had given up on, and through God's chesed, she can once again appreciate. The unwavering love of Ruth's and Boaz's compassion helped move Naomi toward redemption, a path that is now clearly marked by this new child who represents a future in Naomi's previously futureless world.

I grew up in an observant Jewish neighborhood where the smells of challah and chicken permeated the endless apartment house hallways every Friday. When dinner was over, we would walk toward our synagogue for an Oneg Shabbat. That is, most of us would walk the two short blocks toward the singing, tea, and cake. Then there was Joe. He would stand in front of the apartment building, puffing on his Shabbat-forbidden cigarette, greeting us with a smile as we walked by. On Yom Kippur, as we marched down eight flights of stairs to avoid using the elevator, and harder yet, marched back up after hours of fasting and praying, Joe would greet us, pushing the elevator button as he bit into his sandwich. As we munched the last of our Pesach charoset, Joe would wave at us before taking another bite of his croissant. And everyone would shake their heads, and murmur about how much Joe lost in the concentration camps, how we have to understand. And then, when I was fifteen, I walked into shul on Rosh Hashanah and there was Joe—dressed neatly in a white suit, wearing squeaky clean white sneakers, a large embroidered kippah on his head. It seemed that time had stopped. We stood still, amazed, bewildered. "Joe," my dad gently approached him, "what happened?" Joe looked up and held my father's eyes with his, and as tears began to fall, he replied, "Hitler is dead and I have a grandson." The possibility of our redemption from empty husks to fully alive human beings, the possibility of a future in a world we thought had no future, is the miracle of Naomi, and the miracle of Joe.

And who is this child who is said to be the restorer of Naomi's life? He is named Oved, a word whose root means work or service and is often used in connection with service to God. He is the offspring of two people who understood how to live a sacred life, a life brimming with chesed, a life in the service of God. Through this service, turning toward what is right is possible, and redemption is possible. As our story closes, Naomi is nursing Oved, nursing this sacred Service, and thus nursing the future of our people. After all, this baby whom she nurtures will grow to be the grandfather of King David, a king who will unite our people and whose beautiful songs offer our gratitude and service to God to this very day. Naomi spiritually nurses the next generation with her hard earned understanding that if we serve God through our daily actions and behavior toward people, there will be a future and that future will be in a psychological land of milk and honey, a land rich with fields of corn and barley. There is no famine in that internal land if we can live a sacred life, a life marked by chesed. In that sacred space within us, turning, love, redemption, and a hopeful future are all possible.

Notes

1. Tanach stands for "Torah, Neviim and Ketuvim," meaning Torah, Prophets, and Writings. These three books compose the sacred written Torah of the Jewish tradition.

2. Our rabbis are particularly angry at the Moabites because after the Israelites were redeemed from Egypt, they would not meet them with food or water, and then they sent Balaam to curse them (Deut. 23:4, Numbers Rabbah, 11:7).

3. After the destruction of Sodom and Gemorrah, the only survivors of those cities were Abraham's nephew Lot, his wife (who, upon looking back at the destroyed cities, turned into a pillar of salt), and his daughters. After their escape, Lot's daughters were convinced that they were the only ones left alive, and had incestuous relationships with their father in order to continue the human race. The child of one of those relationships was named Moab, meaning "from the father." See Genesis 19:30-38.

4. Rabbi Nosso Scherman is credited with this idea, which is expanded upon by Tamar Frankiel. See for example Frankiel, T. (2001). *The Gift of Kabbalah*, Woodstock, VT: Jewish Lights Publishing, pp. 20-23.

5. Our sages say that Elimelech's death is a punishment for leaving Judah (where Bethlehem is located) in a time of need. He is portrayed as a wealthy, influential man who abandoned his obligation to his neighbors and community (Ruth Rabbah, 1:4)

6. See Ruth 1:1 and 1:4.

7. See Aviva Zornberg's Chapter, specifically the note on p. 66, in *Reading Ruth*, Judith Kates and Gail Reimer, eds., Ballantine Books, NY, 1994.

8. Biblical writer Ruth Sohn notes that, prior to this time, Moab and not Judah was mentioned by name in this text. Now, Judah and not Moab is mentioned. Sohn sees this as a psychological shift. Naomi is now focused on Judah, toward a movement forward rather than simply away from Moab, toward correcting her earlier error of abandoning the land, of leaving the people and place that could nourish her. Sohn, R. (1994). Verse by Verse: A Modern Commentary. In *Reading Ruth,* p. 19.

9. Some rabbis berate Orpah's decision and develop the legend that Orpah becomes the mother of the giant Goliath (Sotah 42b, *The Babylonian Talmud*; Ruth Rabbah 2:20), and that she also went to the land of the Phillistines and had six illegitimate sons, all of whom were killed by David (Zohar Chadash, R. bar Yochai, *The Zohar.*). Goliath, of course, is killed by Ruth's great-grandson, David. One source (Sotah 42b, *The Babylonian Talmud*.) even has God saying that Orpah's descendents will fall before Ruth's descendents because Orpah "kissed" while Ruth "cleaved." Some of our sages think that the name Orpah is derived from the word for back (Oref), supposedly because Orpah turned her back to Naomi and returned home (Zohar Chadash, Ruth 81b; Ruth Rabbah 2:9).

10. The prayer is known as "Eitz Chayim."

11. Ruth 1:16. The pronoun were changed to contemporary form from that in the Koren Publishers Tanach.

12. See Mona Fishbane's chapter in *Reading Ruth.*

13. Ravah, or saturate, is proposed by Rabbi Johanan. Ruth Rabbah suggests that her name comes from ra-ah or "to see" and Gloria Goldreich in her Midrash published in *Reading Ruth:* "Ruth, Naomi, and Orpah: A Parable about Friendship," links Ruth to "re-ut" or friendship. The Gematria, or Jewish study of numbers, tells us that Ruth's name adds up to 613, or the number of Mitzvot incumbent upon Jews.

14. The word "vatayhom" is often translated as "astir," but Aviva Zornberg comments that the word is stronger than that and that it implies panic. (See her chapter in *Reading Ruth.*)

15. Tamar Frankel (see *Reading Ruth*) expounds on a Midrash: Not gleaning in another field means do not glean in another spiritual field. Keeping your

eyes on the field is significant because land reflects the light of Torah. Ruth is also told to stay close to the maidens because the Women of Israel reflect the Shechina.

16. Ruth, 2:11.

17. Ruth Rabbah 1:4 says that Elimelech feared that all his neighbors would come to him for food during the famine, and to avoid this, he left the land.

18. The text can also be read as Boaz is "our redemption."

19. The act of uncovering Boaz's feet is euphemistically sexual in nature. See Nehama Aschkenasy's essay "Language as Female Empowerment in Ruth," in *Reading Ruth*.

20. Koheles Rabbah 10:8 says that while her father and brothers were in the house of study, Dinah went out to look at the daughters of the land, and Sechel Tov, Bereshit 34:1 adds that she went out to show the gentiles her beauty so that they would see that there was none like her among them. See *Encyclopedia of Biblical Personalities*, Yishai Chasidah, Shaar Press, 1994.

21. See Ruth Sohn's work in *Reading Ruth*.

22. It is said that Boaz's name means strength because he fought the evil inclination and did not make sexual advances toward Ruth that night. (Tikkunei Zohar 31:75b, *The Zohar.*)